THE COMPLETE GUIDE TO
AUTO BODY REPAIR
2nd Edition

By Dennis W. Parks

motorbooks

Quarto is the authority on a wide range of topics.

Quarto educates, entertains and enriches the lives of our readers—enthusiasts and lovers of hands-on living.

www.quartoknows.com

First published in 2015 by Motorbooks, an imprint of Quarto Publishing Group USA Inc., 400 First Avenue North, Suite 400, Minneapolis, MN 55401 USA.
Telephone: (612) 344-8100 Fax: (612) 344-8692

quartoknows.com
Visit our blogs at quartoknows.com

Motorbooks titles are also available at discounts in bulk quantity for industrial or sales-promotional use. For details contact the Special Sales Manager at Quarto Publishing Group USA Inc., 400 First Avenue North, Suite 400, Minneapolis, MN 55401 USA.

10 9 8 7 6 5 4 3 2 1

ISBN: 978-0-7603-4945-8

Library of Congress Cataloging-in-Publication Data

Parks, Dennis, 1959-
  The complete guide to auto body repair / Dennis Parks.
    pages cm
Includes bibliographical references and index.
  ISBN 978-0-7603-4945-8 (pb : alk. paper)
  1. Automobiles--Bodies--Maintenance and repair--
Amateurs' manuals. I. Title.
  TL255.P36 2015
  629.2'60288--dc23
                        2015020711

Acquiring Editor: Zack Miller
Project Manager: Alyssa Bluhm
Senior Art Director: Brad Springer
Layout Designer: Laurie Young

Printed in China

On the front cover: Longtime Motorbooks collaborator and auto body repair professional Chad Wyttenbach applies a fresh skim coat of filler prior to sanding on a maroon 1966 Ford Mustang fastback.

Raymond Auto Body
1075 Pierce Butler Route
St. Paul, MN 55104

www.raymondautobody.com
651-488-0588

Contents

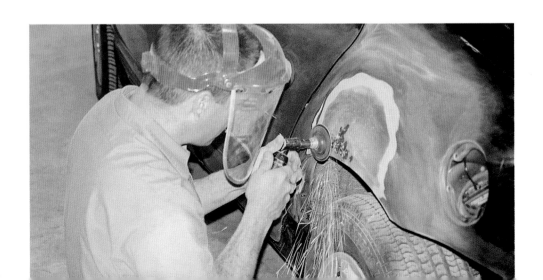

Dedication

To Dad and Aunt Joan, both gone much too soon. I miss you.

Foreword

You're lucky. When I started doing auto bodywork, I didn't have a book like this to help me. My knowledge came from what I learned as I worked and what I learned by asking questions from professional auto body technicians I knew. This was a costly and time-consuming way to go about mastering a new skill. Dennis has prepared a lot of information for you to eliminate much of the learning by trial and error. You have a great head start that I didn't have.

Don't be afraid to start an auto body project, but try to pick a small repair for your first experience. If you do make a mistake, you'll be out some additional expense and the extra time it takes you to redo your work, but you will have learned something. Auto bodywork is a skill learned by doing. Dennis will prepare you with his book, but you actually need hands-on experiences to acquire the skill. As you do more bodywork, you'll get faster and better, but everyone begins with that first job.

A completed auto body repair can bring a feeling of great satisfaction. My goal is to repair the vehicle so that no one can detect the prior damage. A custom or street rod job should be better than the standards of the original equipment manufacture. The body and paint should be smooth, flat, and glossy, and all the body panels should fit as perfect as humanly possible. Set your standards very high and avoid the attitude that substandard work will be okay. After each job, critique your work. Make a mental note of what looks good and what you can do better next time. In auto bodywork, each successive step depends on quality work done on the prior operation. A great paint job can't hide substandard bodywork. Perform each step of the process to the best of your ability, with the tools, skills, and the knowledge you have.

Enjoy your auto body repair experiences. Take pride in your work and take credit for it. Nothing matches the feeling of hearing someone say, "Wow, you did all that work yourself. It looks great."

John Kimbrough

Acknowledgments

A very sincere thank you goes out to everyone who helped with this book—I couldn't have done it without your help. In no particular order, thanks to Jim Miller, Duane Wissman and the staff at Jerry's Auto Body, Donnie and Jack Karg at Karg's Hot Rod Service, Keith Moritz and staff at Morfab Customs, along with Kevin and Wendy Brinkley at The Paint Store.

I also need to thank Roger Ward at Bad Paint Company and John Kimbrough for all the information they've provided over the years and for proofreading my manuscripts.

Dennis W. Parks

Introduction

Even if you aren't a hot rodder, "car guy," or any other type of automobile aficionado, there are times when you need to perform automotive bodywork.

Suppose your recently licensed teenager has just had a fender-bender. You could turn it in to your insurance and have the repair work done at your local body shop. However, ask yourself, "What will this do to my insurance rates?"

Maybe you're a prudent parent and purchase this first-time driver a relatively cheap vehicle and are just carrying liability insurance on it. The car runs well, but it just isn't socially acceptable to your "image-is-everything" teenager. Depending on the amount of damage, you may not be able to pass the car off as brand new. With a little bit of work, though, you can probably make it look better. In the worst-case scenario, you'll at least develop a better understanding of why auto body repair shops charge what they do.

Of course, if you're a car guy (or gal), you may realize that the car of your dreams in perfect condition is beyond your means, but that you can have what you really want if you can restore or modify one that is in less-than-perfect condition. Starting with a rusted-out or dented hulk of a body and then transforming it into the vehicle you've always wanted takes patience and passion—when you've finished your work, it will mean more to you than an already finished vehicle that you bought from someone else.

You could also find a vehicle that works mechanically but needs some tender loving care in the bodywork department. If you can learn to hammer out a few dents and touch up some paint, you can often make some good money buying used cars, doing some minor bodywork, and then selling them. This is a great opportunity if you live in or near a college town where decent-looking used vehicles for sale aren't readily available.

Over the years, the way cars are built has changed a lot, which means that the way to repair these vehicles has also changed. What was once an industry focused on hammering out dents in sheet metal panels now focuses on replace-and-paint techniques, since many auto components are now made of composites that are cheaper to replace than to repair. Still, for many of us, repairing it ourselves is more desirable for a variety of reasons.

My goal with this book is to teach you how to make the necessary repairs to your vehicle, whether the panel to be repaired is metal or a composite. Chapters 1 and 2 discuss the tools and materials you need for performing auto body repair, while Chapter 3 helps you develop a strategy for making the repairs. In Chapter 4 we'll get our hands dirty by disassembling the vehicle as required and determining how best to strip old paint and rust from the parts that need repair. Chapter 5 discusses repairs to metal components, while Chapter 6 deals primarily with composite body panels and their repair. Rust repair is covered in Chapter 7, and Chapters 8 and 9 focus on post-repair surface preparation and paint application, respectively. Chapter 10 concludes the process with a focus on reassembly.

I hope this book gets you motivated about performing your own auto body repair, giving you the confidence to do it yourself.

Chapter 1
Tools

No matter what your task, having the correct tools will make the job easier and yield a better result. However, you don't need every tool the local body shop has to work on your own vehicle. A professional body shop owner saves money by having all the tools on hand that will speed up the process. When it comes to your own bodywork, you don't have to worry so much about time. While you may need to figure out ways to be more versatile with the tools you have, the less money you spend on tools that you'll only use occasionally will leave more cash in your wallet.

Owning—or at least having access to—the correct tools won't make your work any better if you don't apply some practical experience. Don't get me wrong: This doesn't mean you should go out and get yourself into a fender-bender just for bodywork repair experience. Salvage yards have plenty of used fenders and doors that you can buy for practice. If you have a project that requires some bodywork, but you're feeling a little hesitant, you can always buy a dented fender for practice before you start work on a vehicle that you want to fix up.

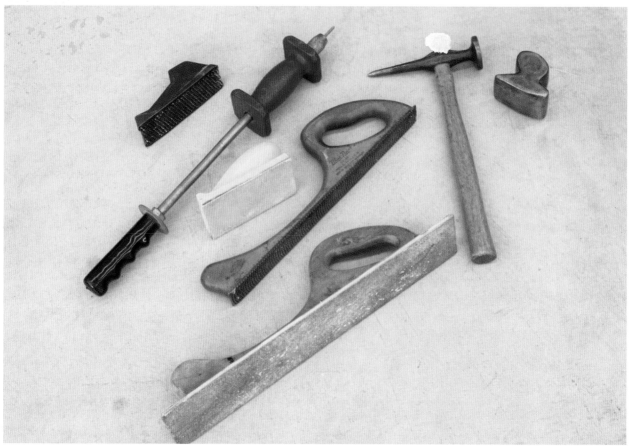

These are some of the basic tools required for performing automotive bodywork. Beginning at the upper left is a cheese-grater type file, a slide hammer, a small sanding block, a lead file, a long sanding board, a body hammer, and a dolly.

Body hammers come in a variety of shapes, sizes, and uses. Those with a serrated head are used for shrinking metal. Round heads are used for general panel flattening, while square heads are used for restoring bodylines.

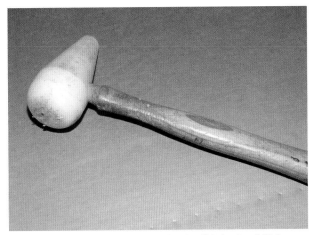

Mallets are typically used for hammer-forming flat sheet metal into custom shapes, and sometimes require the use of a wooden buck against which to hammer the metal.

BASIC TOOLS

As with most professions, there are certain basic tools you need. For automotive bodywork, these include hammers, dollies, sanding boards, grinders, and sanders. You can't really do much bodywork without these basic tools. Spray guns for applying primer and paint are basic, too, but you will find them listed with the pneumatic tools. Besides, this is a book about bodywork. For priming and painting, refer to Motorbooks' *How to Paint Your Car*, by Dennis W. Parks.

Hammers

Leading the list of basic tools are hammers. They may seem truly basic, but there are many types of hammer used for bodywork with specific characteristics and applications. Some situations call for a big hammer, while others require a smaller hammer and a lighter touch. Learning all the types and knowing when to use them can be challenging for amateur body men.

Most body hammers have a head and a pick, making each hammer a dual-purpose tool. The head is usually large (between one and two inches in diameter) and relatively flat with a smooth surface, while the pick end is much smaller and pointed. The larger head is used for flattening metal against a dolly (for more detail on this technique, refer to "Dolly-On/Dolly-Off Hammering" in Chapter 5). Typically, the pick end is used for hammering out very small, localized dents, with or without a dolly. Picks can come to a very narrow point or can be more blunt.

In a collision, sheet metal bends and stretches. A shrinking hammer with a serrated head can be used to reduce some of this stretching.

Different hammer manufacturers combine different heads with different picks. When you buy bodywork hammers, look for a set that includes a flat face, a shrinking face, a blunt pick, and a sharp pointed pick. This range should be enough for you to handle most of your hammering needs.

Mallets

Mallets differ from bodywork hammers in construction material and shape, as well as how they are used. A mallet's striking surface is usually made of plastic or some other composite that will not mar sheet metal or aluminum. Mallets are available in different sizes and may be cylindrical or teardrop-shaped. While you typically use a hammer to return damaged auto body sheet metal to a preformed shape, mallets are designed to hammer flat sheet metal into a custom shape.

Dollies

Made of smooth, hardened steel, dollies come in a variety of shapes and sizes. Dollies are usually held on the backside of the metal being straightened, while a hammer on the outside flattens the metal between the two, resulting in metal that is roughly the shape of the portion of the dolly being used. For this reason, having a number of different dollies with small, large,

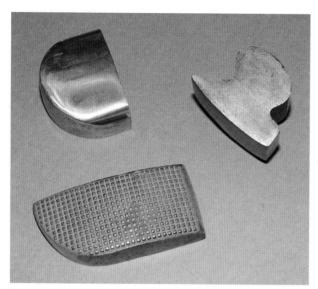

Just like hammers, dollies also come in a variety of shapes and sizes. A wider variety of shapes will enable you to recreate original bodylines more precisely and more easily. At the upper left is a toe dolly with increasing and decreasing radii, at right is a general-purpose dolly with a variety of shapes, and at the bottom is a serrated dolly for shrinking metal.

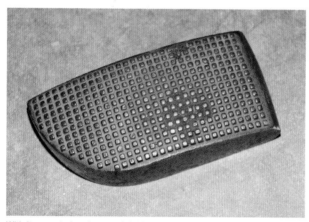

With its serrated surface, a shrinking dolly (shown) or shrinking hammer can be used to shrink metal that is stretched in a collision. Hammering the metal against or with the serrated surface causes the material to bunch up, thereby shrinking it.

convex, and concave shapes will add to your versatility. Like shrinking hammers, dollies with a serrated face help shrink stretched metal.

Spoons

Designed for use inside hard-to-reach areas, spoons function like a body dolly with a handle. Often smaller and thinner than a dolly, they can be used inside of doors, fenders, hoods, or other double wall panels. They can also be used for prying panels outward from behind.

Sanding Blocks

Sanding blocks are commercially available in a wide variety of shapes, styles, sizes, and materials. You can also use improvised sanding blocks, whose range is pretty much unlimited. No matter how good you get at straightening damaged sheet metal, the finished paint simply will not look its best unless you exert enough effort to make the surface smooth and flat. Sanding can help you get the best results, but without a sanding block you'll be wasting your time.

These are just a few of the many types and sizes of sanding boards. The three Flexsand boards are middle-of-the-road in terms of stiffness. They secure the sandpaper with hook-and-loop backing. The two sanding boards with hardwood handles are the stiffest and therefore are best for large, flat surfaces. They secure the sandpaper with a spring clip. The small rubber block at the lower right is the most flexible. Sandpaper fits into a slot on each end and is secured with a couple of tacks that are part of the block.

Sanding blocks help you exert even pressure on the sandpaper, while minimizing waves in the panel being sanded. Since automotive body panels come in a variety of contours, there are different requirements for sanding blocks. If the panel has lots of curves or round surfaces, the sanding block needs to be flexible but firm in order to maintain contact between the body surface and the sandpaper. Sanding blocks are made out of rubber or various types of foam, which allow them to be flexible. Some sanding blocks are designed with removable rods that slide into or out of

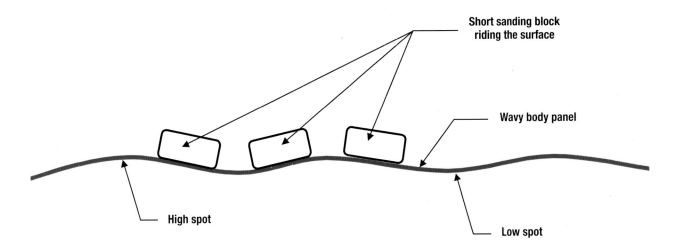

Short sanding block
riding the surface

Wavy body panel

High spot

Low spot

Besides smoothing the surface, part of the reason for sanding is to make wavy panels flat. A short sanding board or block can be used to get any panel smooth, but it will not necessarily get the panel flat. A short sanding board or block will merely ride over the ridges, rather than knocking them down.

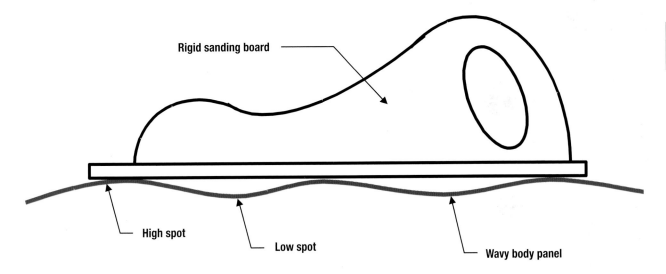

Rigid sanding board

High spot

Low spot

Wavy body panel

By using the longest sanding board possible for the area being sanded, the sandpaper will span across the ridges in a body panel and quickly knock down the ridges, making the panel flat as well as smooth.

the back; these help you fine-tune the block's flexibility by stiffening the block with more rods, making it more flexible with less, and so on.

On the other hand, if you are sanding a flat surface (such as a hood or roof panel), a more rigid sanding board may be appropriate. The more rigid and longer the board, the more effective it will be in eliminating waves in the panel. A longer board will span across multiple ripples, working to knock down the high spots where a short sanding block simply skims across the surface.

Although most sanding blocks and boards have a flat surface, some sanding boards are designed with a concave surface, allowing you to smooth the inside of a curved surface. These are available in a variety of radii.

Whenever you purchase sanding boards or blocks, you should take special notice of how the sandpaper is held in place, as not all sandpaper is compatible with all sanding boards and blocks. Small, inexpensive rubber sanding blocks often have a horizontal slit in both ends, with the top flap and two or three sharp tacks to grab the sandpaper. The sandpaper is wrapped around the bottom of the block, with the ends of the paper placed between the upper and lower flap held in place by the tacks. Some sanding boards have spring clips that hold the paper in place, while others use adhesive-backed sandpaper.

Portable Grinders and Sanders

For most do-it-yourself repairs, sending a panel to be media-blasted or chemically stripped isn't feasible. A sander or grinder is a must-have tool for the quick removal of paint, primer, and old body filler from an area being repaired. These tools are available in electric or pneumatic models, and in different sizes, motor speeds, and price ranges.

You have a choice between an electric sander and a pneumatic model. If you don't own an air compressor, an electric sander will suffice, since your shop is most likely small enough to allow for an extension cord to reach electric outlets. If you already have an air compressor that can maintain a large volume of air, a pneumatic model may serve your purposes better. Pneumatic sanders can withstand longer, nonstop use, while electric models have a tendency to overheat. When it overheats, an electric sander's motor will shut down; you can get the sander going again by pressing a reset switch, but this can lead to inconvenient interruptions as you work.

If you'll be working on a large area of the vehicle, a larger sanding surface will be better, but a smaller workspace (such as around door handles, trim, or other obstacles) will limit how much room you'll have for sanding. Smaller, high-speed grinders and larger speed sanders with a slower speed have worked well for this author. Both can be equipped with sanding discs for removing paint. The relatively small grinder (around 4 inches) can be equipped with a grinding disc for work on heavy metal, such as that found on chassis, while the

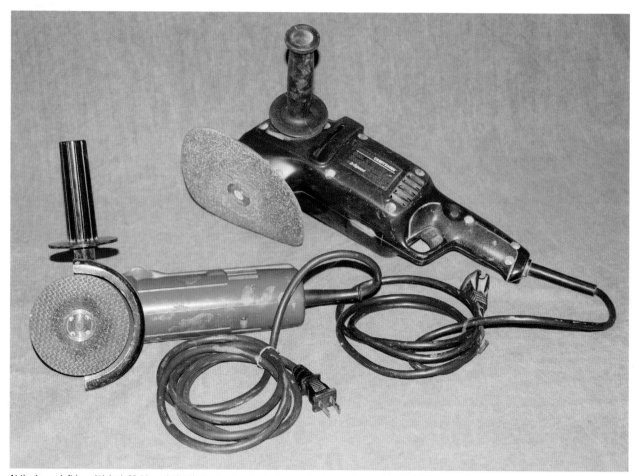

At the lower left is a 4½-inch Makita grinder that can use a rigid grinding disc for grinding welds. It will also accept a wire cup brush, which is useful for removing old body filler or paint. The larger unit is a 7-inch Craftsman sander/buffer. With sanding discs of various grits, this can be used to clean welds or remove old paint or body filler. It can also be fitted with a buffing bonnet to apply wax to finished paint.

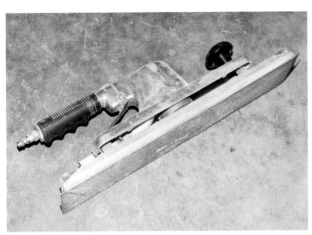

Pneumatic sanding boards that move in a straight line are very useful for block sanding body filler and get it flat. However, they should not be used for removing paint or surface rust, as an orbital sander/grinder would be more appropriate.

7-inch sander can be equipped with a polishing bonnet for buffing and polishing operations.

Stud Welders and Slide Hammers

Pulling out dents in sheet metal has become much easier with the advent of electric stud welders. This tool spot welds a metal pin to the sheet metal panel: the more complex the dent, the more pins need to be used.

After the pins are installed, a slide hammer is clamped onto each pin individually. The pin is then pulled by

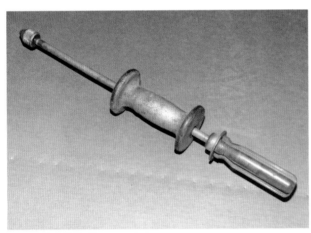

A slide hammer is used for pulling out dents in sheet metal. Earlier designs used small screws that were threaded into tiny holes drilled in the sheet metal, whereas most body shops now use a stud gun that quickly spot welds a metal pin to the sheet metal. In either case, the small end of the slide hammer is tightened onto the screw or pin. With one hand on the handle and the other hand on the hammer (sliding portion), the hammer is slid back in a quick motion, pulling the sheet metal with it.

quickly sliding the cylindrical "hammer" outward along the shaft of the slide hammer. This method pulls the sheet metal back into its original shape. The pins are then cut off and further bodywork (using hammer and dolly, body filler, or other methods) can be performed to complete the repair.

The slide hammer technique has been used for a long time. Before stud welders became available, it was a complicated process. Small holes would be drilled into the sheet metal, then a screw was threaded partially into the hole. After the slide hammer was used to pull the dent, a bunch of small holes would be left in the repaired panel, which weakened the panel and became a starting point for rust. To avoid this, you would have to weld all of the holes you had made shut. Without an electric stud welder, using a slide hammer often created more issues than it repaired.

Door Skin Installer and Removal Pliers

Door skins are typically held in place by folding the edge of the outer door skin (sheet metal) over the edge of the inner door structure. Some automobile designs have the skin spot welded on—this can make door skins easy to remove and replace, but having the correct tools on hand will help. The skin is removed by drilling out the spot welds, if applicable, and then prying the sheet metal away from the door frame. A pry bar or screwdriver can work for this, but the process will go faster and a lot easier if you have specially designed door-skin removal pliers. These usually cost around $30, and they'll pay for themselves in the time you save after skinning just a few doors.

Conversely, door-skin installer pliers are designed to fold the edge of the door skin over the door frame. These pliers cost more, but they create a more uniform fold and don't run the risk of denting the door-skin, which is something you have to watch for when using a hammer.

Panel Flangers

Whenever you're attaching two panels to each other, you will find it useful to create a flange on a piece of sheet metal. Rather than simply butting the edges of the two panels together, a flange on one piece allows it to fit behind the second piece, yet still have an edge to abut. The two pieces can then be plug welded together or attached with rivets, depending on the application.

Panel-flanging tools are available in two basic styles, as a bead roller through which the sheet metal is fed, or as clamping pliers that are used manually. The bead-roller style can be found as inexpensive models that clamp into a bench vise, or as a standalone unit. The price will vary, depending on whether you choose a hand-crank model or one with a motor to feed the sheet metal through, as well as the model's capacity to handle metals of varying thickness. Regardless of style or size, the sheet metal is fed between two mandrels, each mounted to the end of two long cylinders. The shape of the machined mandrels gives the sheet metal its new shape. Each flanging mandrel has two differently sized diameters to create the flange. A bead mandrel works similarly, but in this model one mandrel has a cylindrical shape with a convex ring around it near the end, while its mating mandrel has a concave ring aligned with the convex ring, resulting in a raised bead in the sheet metal.

Manual flangers operate like locking pliers. The heads of the pliers are stepped (similar to the flanging mandrel), creating a flange when the sheet metal is clamped between the jaws of the pliers. This style requires flanging the sheet metal in one location, releasing the pliers, moving them along the edge being flanged, and then flanging again. If you need to make multiple flanges, this can take longer, but manual flangers are much cheaper than the bead roller type.

PNEUMATIC TOOLS

Pneumatic tools can do more than just spray primer and paint. In fact, air-powered tools can perform most

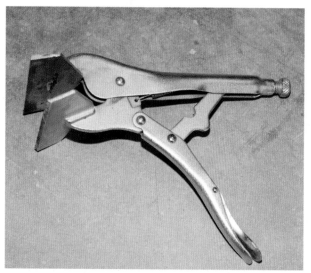

Duckbill clamps are not actually used for making flanges on sheet metal, but they are useful for straightening or bending existing flanges. They can also clamp mounting flanges while welding the two pieces together.

of the same functions as the basic hand-operated tools reviewed above—except much faster. That's a good thing, since you'll have more time to concentrate on detailed finish work (if you are so inclined), and you will be less fatigued at the end of a work session.

Remember, though, that using power tools won't guarantee that you'll do a better job. If you don't know what you're doing, using a pneumatic sander or grinder will get you into trouble a whole lot faster than if you were sanding by hand.

You should also realize that the speed and ease of pneumatic tools comes with a price. If you are an automotive hobbyist, the price might be reasonable, especially if you foresee other automotive projects in your future. If you are simply trying to make a one-time repair, you may be better off buying or borrowing the hand tools you need to make the repair—even if it means having the paint work done by Maaco or some other repaint shop. The choice is up to you.

Air Compressor

Most professional paint shops use an air compressor rated at a minimum of 10 horsepower (hp), often much larger. These big units supply plenty, allowing workers to operate pneumatic tools and painting equipment at the same time. For the hobbyist, a smaller compressor may be enough, as long as the compressor is rated at 4 horsepower or greater and has a tank that is at least 25 gallons in size.

Horsepower is not the only important criterion for an air compressor: the size of the tank is at least as critical for repair work of this kind. This is because the more a compressor works, the hotter the air supply becomes. As the heat continues to increase, moisture condenses inside the equipment's piping and enters the compressor's air system. In order to avoid this situation, your air compressor should be able to build up a reserve of compressed air in its holding tank, then shut off as it cools down.

You can determine the size of air compressor you need by comparing the required cubic feet per minute (cfm) of air needed for your pneumatic tools with the cfm rating on the compressor you plan to use. If the compressor can easily supply the required cfm at the prescribed application pressure, you should have no problem.

Your compressor must also have adequate capacity for the job. For example, a 5 horsepower compressor with a 20-gallon tank that supplies enough air for a conventional spray gun may be enough to keep up with the demands of a high-volume, low-pressure (HVLP) production paint guns. Instead, the recommendation is for a hose size of 5/16 inch inside diameter in maximum lengths of 25 feet. For HVLP spray guns, a 3/8-inch inside diameter air hose is recommended. As long as you are using compatible hoses and couplings and have a compressor of sufficient size, the larger the diameter air hose, the better. With the exception of those used for commercial-grade sand blasters, most air hoses found in a body repair paint shop will be 3/4 inch in diameter or less.

Regulators

Ensure that you have the air pressure required for proper use in your air tools by holding the trigger wide open while adjusting the air pressure regulator controls. Although a control gauge setting might show 40 pounds per square inch (psi) while in a static condition, operating your air tools may cause this reading to drop to 30 or

If you are going to use pneumatic tools, you'll need plenty of compressed air. This commercial unit requires 240-volt electric service, and has a 60-gallon air tank. For use in your home garage, you may be better off finding a 110-volt unit unless you have extra electric service installed. Whichever you choose, get the largest tank you can afford and can fit in your workspace.

spray gun. Instead of being able to spray a complete coat of paint at one time, you may have to stop in the middle of your job (or several times) to allow the air supply to catch up. The same 5 horsepower compressor with a 35-gallon tank may be more appropriate when using an HVLP tool. Likewise, when using other high-demand pneumatic tools, such as a plasma cutter or sander, a tank with a larger capacity will prevent frequent stops to let the air compressor catch up with you.

Hoses and Couplings

False pressure gauge readings can occur if you are using the wrong size air hose for your tools' air supply. Small-diameter hoses can experience friction loss, causing pressures to dwindle when the air travels from the air compressor to the tool being powered. PPG's *Refinish Manual* suggests 1/4-inch hose is too small for standard

Pressure regulators between the air compressor and the tool being used are essential. This particular model has an air supply line entering from the right, and is used to regulate two separate lines that exit from the left. Sanders, grinders, and air saws require a certain amount of air to operate properly, while spray guns must be operated within a specific air pressure range depending on the material being applied.

35 psi. Most pneumatic tools are designed to work most efficiently at a particular airflow rate that varies from one piece of equipment to another. If your air compressor can't provide enough air, your tools won't function as efficiently as they should. Most important, though, is that you apply auto paint at the psi rating indicated on the container label or in the product's application guide literature.

Driers/Filters

A clean, dry, controlled source of air pressure for any spray paint job is *essential* (yes, this applies to working with primer, too). If moisture and/or dirt accumulates and eventually exits a spray gun's nozzle, the finish will be blemished with fisheyes, dirt nibs, and possibly blushing problems all over the surface. Additionally, minuscule particles of water, oil, or rust can find their way from holding tanks to other air-powered tools unless they are captured and retained somewhere between the compressor and equipment being used.

You could buy the most expensive auto paint products available, spend weeks and weeks preparing your car or truck's surface to perfection, use the most highly advanced spray paint gun available—and *still* ruin your paint job with an inadequate air compressor or a holding tank gunked up with moisture and oil residue. You can also ruin your other pneumatic tools if you allow them to take in moist air, since this may cause the internal components to rust, greatly shortening their useful life.

After you've figured out which air compressor to use, consider installing a piping system with a water trap or air drier located at one end. Even for home use, a small air supply system with a ¾-inch to 1-inch pipe can be helpful, opposed to merely connecting the air supply hose to the air compressor's outlet. A copper or galvanized pipe running downhill, away from a compressor toward a water trap or dryer, will allow moisture accumulations in heated air to flow away from the compressor and toward the trap or dryer. Since the hot air will have time to cool inside the pipes, any moisture suspended in the air will condense into droplets that can be captured and retained as a liquid in the trap.

Do-it-yourself body men can run ¾- to 1-inch copper or galvanized pipe up from the location of the compressor to the ceiling, then attach a horizontal section to the riser and run it slightly downhill toward the opposite end of the garage or workshop. Another section then runs down the wall to a convenient point where a water trap or air dryer can be mounted. Working air lines connect at the trap or dryer for use with pneumatic tools or spray guns.

To keep portable air compressors mobile and prevent their operational vibration from causing damage to solid piping mounted to walls, you should connect your compressor to the piping system with a short, flexible air hose. This allows you to disconnect the air compressor from the piping system easily, then move it to wherever you need it for other jobs.

Spray Guns

Even if you don't expect to apply paint, you will need to apply primers and other substrates during the bodywork repair stage. Spray guns, available in a variety of designs and a very broad price range, are the tools to use for this purpose.

Before purchasing a spray gun, you should determine if you will use traditional paint products (solvent-based) or a new, waterborne paint. You may have heard rumors about waterborne paint products, but bear in mind that they are not mandatory everywhere and, in fact, they can be hard to find in areas where they are not required. Waterborne paints are required in parts of Europe for some time, and they are also becoming a requirement in California. However, the general consensus is that waterborne paints will not be required outside of these restricted areas until around the end of the first quarter of the twenty-first century (i.e., 2025).

Other than requiring different air pressures, waterborne paints are applied just like solvent-based paints. Spray guns that are compatible for waterborne paints utilize stainless steel or other materials that won't cause rust in the sprayer's internal parts. Again, unless you are in an area that currently requires waterborne paint, you most likely will not be affected by this for another 20 or so years. Throughout the rest of this book, methods and equipment will apply to both solvent-based and waterborne paint, unless specifically designated as one or the other.

HVLP

The introduction of waterborne paint into the market has eliminated most of the issues associated with solvents and volatile organic compounds (VOCs) found in paint products. Until the use of waterborne paint is required everywhere, HVLP spray guns are arguably the next best thing for handling VOCs. As the name implies, these

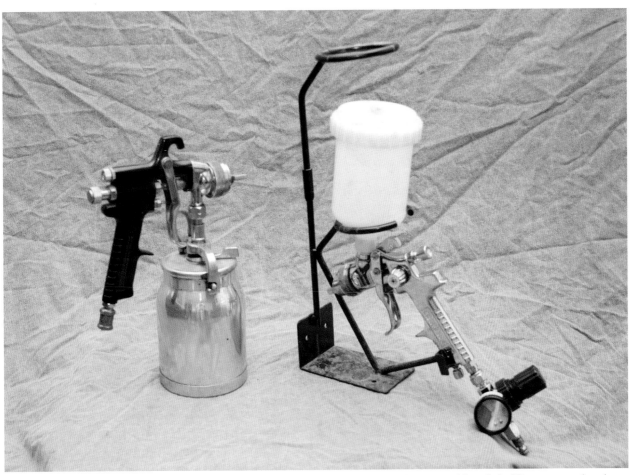

At left is a conventional siphon feed spray gun, while the one on the right is an HVLP (high-volume, low-pressure) type. Each of these were purchased new for around $100 each, although they were on the inexpensive end of the spectrum. However, unless you are painting vehicles on a daily basis, these will probably suit your purpose.

spray guns deliver paint by using a higher volume of air at a lower pressure than conventional spray guns. Anyone who has used a conventional spray gun is probably familiar with the cloud of overspray that occurs. This overspray is the result of the paint material bouncing off the surface, since it is being applied at high pressure. By applying the paint at a lower pressure with an HVLP spray gun, more paint stays on the target surface, resulting in more efficient coverage, less polluted overspray, and less overall material consumption.

Conventional (Suction-Feed)

Conventional or suction-feed spray guns are slowly disappearing from the marketplace. Their design calls for higher air pressure to pull the paint from the cup and propel it toward the surface being painted. This high air pressure causes much of the paint to bounce off the target surface, resulting in inefficient overspray.

Although suction-feed guns can give excellent results, HVLP guns apply the paint much more efficiently.

Conventional guns became less expensive with the advent of HVLP spray guns. However, HVLP guns are now available for similar prices. The amount of material saved when applying paint with an HVLP spray gun, versus a conventional gun, will quickly make up for any additional price for purchasing this equipment.

Full-Size

Full-size spray guns are designed for use when applying primer or paint to large areas, such as a fender, door, or entire vehicle. Designed either for HVLP or suction-feed functionality, these spray guns typically have a paint cup that holds about a quart or liter of sprayable material. Full-size spray guns can be used to spray substrates such as primer or top coats (paint or clear).

At left is a full-size HVLP spray gun alongside a much smaller detail (or jamb) gun. The larger gun has a 1-liter capacity cup and is used to apply primer or paint to large areas. The detail gun is used to apply primer or paint to small areas or, more commonly, to confined areas where a full-size gun would be difficult to maneuver.

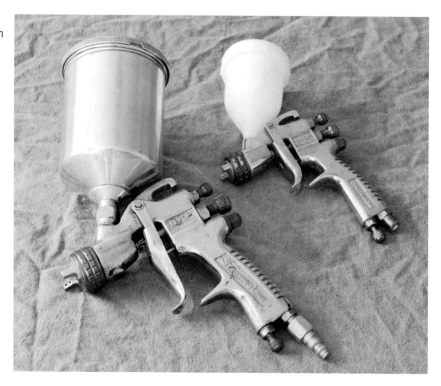

Fluid Tip Sizes

The size of the fluid tip determines the type of material a spray gun can distribute, and the air pressure required to do so. Primers and other substrates are typically thicker than top coats (paint and clear), while heavy coatings such as bed liner material are thicker still. These thick materials require a fluid tip of about 2.2 mm in size, while primer can be sprayed through a fluid tip that is between 1.5 and 1.8 mm. Base coats and clear top coats can usually be sprayed with fluid tips between 1.2 and 1.5 mm in size.

You should purchase a spray gun with a tip that is compatible for what you will be spraying. Most spray guns have removable fluid tips, but they are sold with just one size tip included. However, some spray guns include different size fluid tips. If you're doing a lot of bodywork and painting, you will probably be better off to purchase one gun for spraying primer and another for spraying top coats. If you have a one-time project, though, a single spray gun with multiple tips may be enough to serve your purposes.

Detail

Detail spray guns are also known as "jamb guns," because they are particularly suited for spraying in confined areas such as doorjambs. They can be used to spray primer or top coats. A jamb gun's paint cup will be much smaller than that of a full-size spray gun, so using this kind of spray gun for painting or priming an entire panel will require you to fill the paint cup several times.

Cutting Tools

Before installing a patch panel in sheet metal, you should cut out the area that is being replaced, whether due to rust, severe collision damage, or for some other reason. If the rusty portion of sheet metal is not removed, the rust will extend to the new sheet metal over time. In addition, damaged sheet metal must be removed for the replacement to fit correctly.

Air Chisel

An air chisel is ideal for quick and easy removal of rivets or stripped bolts in chassis or other heavy metal objects. Air chisels can also be used to cut through sheet metal quickly, for example when removing a quarter panel prior to the installation of a new panel. These tools consume a lot of air: if you think you'll make regular use of an air chisel, buy or rent a larger capacity air compressor for the best results.

Die Grinder

For making relatively straight cuts in sheet metal, a die grinder with a cutoff wheel works very well. Most commercially available patch panels have straight edges, so using a die grinder allows you to cut out a similar shape quite easily. Be sure to leave about a half inch of the old metal to overlap the patch panel, and the new panel can then be plug welded in place.

Although they operate the same and perform the same task, die grinders are available in two distinctly different configurations. In both types, the air hose attaches to the end of the die grinder's body, with the body serving as the handle and a lever-type trigger squeezing against the body during operation. The difference in the two styles is that on one, the grinding wheel rotates perpendicular to the body of the die grinder, while on the other the grinding head is mounted at 90 degrees to the body. If you have plenty of room in which to work, this shouldn't pose a problem; however, when space is limited, a die grinder with an angled head is usually more maneuverable.

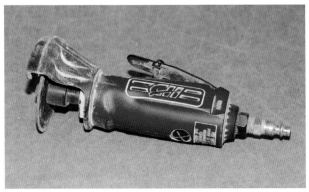

This pneumatic die grinder can be used to make straight cuts in metal. It is typically used as a cutoff tool for small material or to cut out old metal where a patch panel will be installed. Prices range from less than $50 up to about $100.

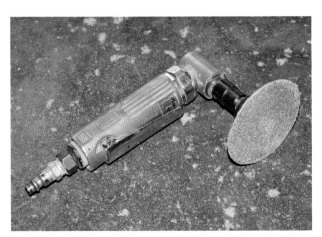

An angle-head grinder works the same as an ordinary die grinder, but with its angled head this tool can sometimes be used in areas that are inaccessible for an ordinary die grinder, depending on the air hose's flexibility.

Reciprocating Air Saw

Anyone who has used a jigsaw or a scroll saw for woodworking will recognize the way a reciprocating air saw works; it is roughly the equivalent tool for use on sheet metal. With a blade that moves back and forth, a reciprocating saw can cut curves or straight cuts in sheet metal, offering more versatility than a die grinder. These are typically used for cutting metal that is still attached to the vehicle, such as when removing rusted or damaged areas that will be replaced with a patch panel.

Shears

Bench-mounted or portable metal shears work in much the same way as scissors: two or more blades act against each other to cut the metal. A long arm and ratchet or gear mechanism works to ease the process of cutting sheet metal. Shears can be used to cut custom patch panels from a piece of flat sheet metal, before welding the piece to the vehicle.

Having a narrow, replaceable reciprocating blade makes a reciprocating air saw good for making freeform cuts in sheet metal.

Nibblers

Nibblers are usually hand-operated (much like scissors), and therefore offer limited applications to thinner sheet metal (as opposed to shears). These tools feature a compound leverage mechanism, making them quick and easy to use—as long as you work within their limits.

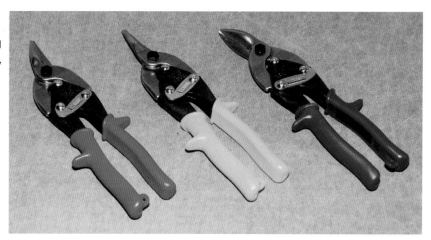

These are compound leverage snips, commonly known as aviation snips. They are used to cut freeform shapes in light metal. The green-handled pair is designed to cut straight or toward the right, while the red-handled pair is designed to cut straight or toward the left. The yellow pair in the middle is designed to cut straight.

Plasma Cutter

Powered by a combination of compressed air and electricity, plasma cutters can cut most anything. However, they are not suitable for cutting through multiple layers of material at one time. The only limiting factor for a plasma cutter is the metal's thickness, which varies by model and the material you wish to cut. With a cutting head that resembles a MIG welding torch, you simply place the head on the material to be cut, squeeze the trigger, and then pull the head along the line you are cutting. Plasma cutters can be used freehand, but they provide a more precise cut if you follow a pattern.

A word of caution: plasma cutters use an incredibly hot arc to melt the material they are cutting. This means that they can cut through virtually anything, including fingers.

A plasma cutter is used like a cutting torch, though a plasma cutter provides a much more precise arc. This minimizes the amount of "finish" work required after the initial work of cutting is completed. A cutting torch may still be used on occasion, especially for doing the rough amputation of a portion of a chassis or quarter panel from a donor vehicle. When the final cutting to size is done, however, a plasma cutter will provide more accurate cuts.

When using a plasma cutter or welder around glass or anything flammable, you should use a welding curtain. Sparks of any kind can damage glass or ignite flammable materials.

Spot Weld Drill Bit

Any time that you are disassembling metal panels that were spot welded together, a spot-weld drill bit and a drill motor will help immensely. Since spot welds are extremely hard, use a slow speed and take your time to reduce premature failure of the spot-weld drill bit.

Requiring electric power, an electric ground, and a good supply of dry, compressed air, a plasma arc cutter will cut virtually anything. Larger, more expensive units can cut thicker materials; however, relatively inexpensive units can cut sheet metal and other materials up to about ¼-inch thick quite handily.

Panel Flangers

Although they may be too expensive for purchase when performing a one-time collision repair, many professional shops have pneumatic panel flangers. At least one type of pneumatic panel flanger also punches holes in sheet metal, which is very useful if you are going to be plug (spot) welding panels together.

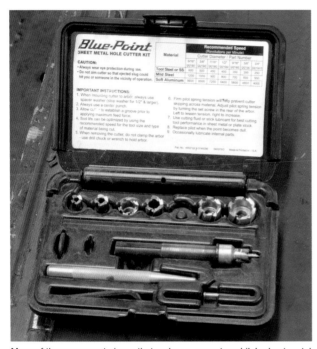

Many of the component pieces that make up our automobile's sheet metal are spot welded together at the factory. If and when those panels require separation, such as when repairing rust, the spot welds must be drilled out. While an ordinary drill bit of the necessary size can be used, the correct tools will make the job much easier.

STANDALONE TOOLS

The following standalone tools are more commonly found in shops where professional or serious amateurs do bodywork. Some items are expensive, while others can be reasonably priced. You won't need them for every task, but there is no doubt that having them can make your job easier.

Welders

Welding is the best way to join two or more pieces of metal permanently. While tried-and-true rivets offer an alternative to welding, they can vibrate loose, making them less desirable for automotive applications. Most metals used in automotive bodywork are steel and aluminum, which can be welded with either MIG or TIG

When plug welding, such as for patch panel installation, one panel must have a small hole in it prior to every weld. Rather than drilling each hole, this pneumatic panel flanger punches a hole at a press of the lever.

This pneumatic panel flanger also presses a flange into the sheet metal by inserting the sheet metal into the opposite side of the head and pressing the operating lever. This method may take longer than using a bead-rolling type flanger, but this type is more versatile for accessibility.

After just a minute or two with the pneumatic flanger, both of these pieces of sheet metal have been flanged, allowing them to be aligned more easily and welded together.

welding. Stainless steel, copper, or brass can also be welded with either method. MIG welding is undoubtedly easier to learn, while TIG welding provides the highest quality and the most aesthetic weld beads. For more information regarding welders and welding, refer to MBI's *Performance Welding Handbook* by Richard Finch.

MIG

MIG welders are ideal for welding patch panels in place. They are easy to learn to use properly, more than adequate for sheet metal work, and affordable. Many models require only 115 volts, making them great for home use. These single-phase models can typically weld up to ⅜-inch thick metal, which is all you will need for most auto body repairs. Larger models that require three-phase electric service are used mainly in production or fabrication shops, or in applications that require welding metal that is thicker than ⅜ inch.

Some additional benefits of MIG welding are relatively high-speed welding, good control on thin metals, and very little weld splatter. Although you will need to skip around some to avoid warping the metal due to heat buildup, being able to lay down a great deal of weld bead in a short time will save you time on a repair. Being able to easily control the heat will allow thorough weld penetration without burning through relatively thin sheet metal body panels. Little to no weld splatter means less cleanup prior to adding body filler or primer/paint applications.

TIG

For automotive uses, TIG welding is more suited to heavy chassis fabrication or repair than to light sheet metal work. It is certainly more difficult to learn, but in the hands of an experienced welder TIG can yield a beautiful weld that requires little if any cleanup afterward.

In addition to providing more precise welds, TIG welding can be used to weld titanium or magnesium alloys. You will probably not be welding these types of material on a daily basis, but a MIG welder is less well suited to completing tasks of this kind properly or as efficiently. On the downside when considering using MIG versus TIG, TIG welding is generally slower and requires more practice to master. However, once you master TIG welding, you can weld virtually any type of metal.

For installing patch panels, fabricating brackets, or any other bodywork chores, nothing beats a MIG welder. Although larger units are available for welding thicker and/or more exotic metals, units perfectly suitable for bodywork chores operate on typical a 110-volt household electric supply. Along with a tank of compressed gas, the proper safety equipment, and a little practice, you can be on your way to becoming an accomplished welder in no time.

Work Stands

For many bodywork repairs, no panels are removed from the vehicle. However, if you must remove a door, fender, hood, deck lid, or bumper from the vehicle to repair that panel, having a work stand or work bench on which to place it will help greatly. Performing bodywork on a fender while it is sitting on the garage floor is simply impractical. Whether you purchase a commercially available work stand or make your own, be sure to put some padding on it so you don't scratch or dent the panel as you work.

TOOLS

For doing any kind of work on a fender or door, a folding work stand is very helpful. It is typically much easier to fill, sand, and paint while you are standing up, rather than lying on the ground. You can find these at swap meets for around $25 or through tool supply stores for a little more. For temporary or one-time use, you could easily make your own out of any tubing you have lying around.

TOOLS

Locking clamps are very common in most any body shop. These are being used to clamp the outer wheelhouse of an early Camaro to the newly replaced quarter panel.

Called intergrip clamps or sheet metal clamps, these work great when butt welding two pieces of sheet metal together. When access to the backside of the sheet metal is available, loosening the wing nut allows removal of the square piece of bar. The remaining tab is inserted between the two pieces of sheet metal, then the square bar is reinstalled and tightened in place. If the backside is not accessible, the clamp can be slid between the two pieces from one edge. The sheet metal can be tack welded together, then the clamps removed.

Clamps

Bar clamps, spring clamps, locking pliers, and C-clamps all have their uses when performing bodywork. It would be impossible to describe all of the uses for clamps, but when you need one—or several—you'll know it.

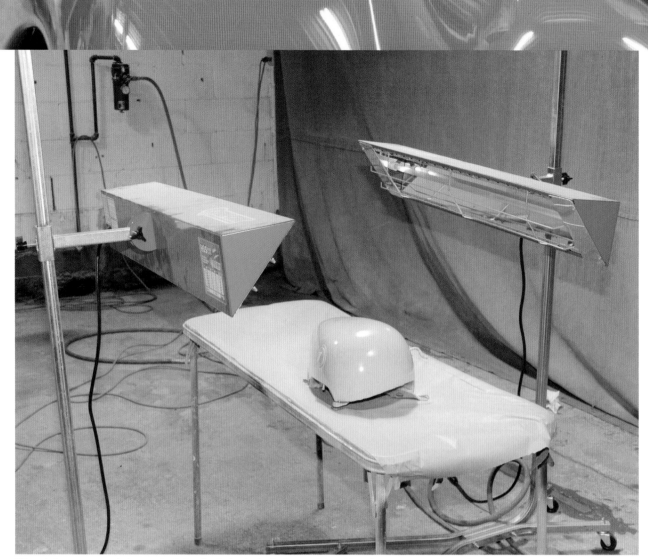

Although they are somewhat expensive to buy for the beginning body man, infrared heat lamps can speed up curing times for plastic filler or speed the paint's drying process. You must make sure that you don't speed up the process too much. If you're pressed for time, though, these can help you out.

Infrared (IR) Heat Lamps

For a one-time repair, heat lamps are an expensive luxury. That said, they are handy if you are pressed for time and need to dry-primer or paint in a short time. Heat lamps can also be used to accelerate the cure time of plastic body filler.

Shrinkers/Stretchers

These are used most often for fabricating curved pieces of metal angle, such as windshield frames, wheelwell edges, and frameworks for trunk openings. They are usually pedestal mounted and can be operated manually or pneumatically.

THE COST OF TOOLS

In general, tools come in a wide variety of qualities and purchase prices. For many guys and gals who make their living with their bodywork and mechanic tools, they would consider nothing less than buying from Snap-On or any of the other expensive tool distributors that serve repair shops. These are no doubt high-quality tools, but they do come with an expensive price tag.

Do you really need to pay a high price for a screwdriver or wrench, when a less expensive one will perform the same task just as well? It's up to you whether you purchase tools from Sears or from Harbor Freight Tools, but ask yourself if you will use the tools you're buying every day or infrequently. It may be nice to have an expensive widget remover, but if you don't use it regularly, does it make more sense to buy from a less expensive distributor and get both the widget installer *and* the widget remover for the same amount of money?

Chapter 2
Materials

You use hammers, dollies, sanders, and welders to straighten, smooth, and join metal, but there are many other components involved in bodywork repair. Some, like paint stripper and body filler, can be applied by hand and require very few tools. Others include the various primers and sealers that serve as a base for the final paint, typically applied with a spray gun driven by compressed air.

HAND APPLICATIONS

Most of the material products associated with auto body repair contain solvents or other chemicals that can cause irritation or worse if your skin comes in direct contact. For this reason, you should always read the warning labels accompanying these materials before using them. Even if the warnings don't suggest wearing disposable gloves, it is a good habit to develop. Disposable gloves are inexpensive, and wearing them sure beats picking fiberglass resin or body filler out of your fingers and cuticles.

Paint Stripper

Paint stripper removes old paint from steel parts and some other metals. Since this product may not be suitable for use on all metals or finishes, you should consult your paint supplier for recommendations on which products to use. Klean-Strip Aircraft® Paint Remover is one brand commonly used for stripping paint from automobiles, and other brands are also available.

Even though chemical stripping does not involve acid (as some people believe), it does involve handling chemicals that require some care in their use and disposal. Chemical paint strippers are safe to use if handled with care: follow the appropriate safety precautions to prevent burns to your skin or other skin irritations.

Wax and Grease Remover

Be sure that the surface you are working on is as clean as possible before sanding, priming, or painting it. All traces of dirt, grease, oil, silicone, or other contaminants must be removed. If the surface is not clean prior to sanding, you run the risk of smearing any contaminants

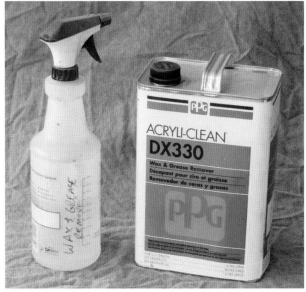

Wax and grease remover is essential for cleaning the surface prior to sanding or spraying undercoats or top coats. Rather than pouring the cleaner onto a cloth or paper towel, invest in a cheap spray bottle to apply the wax and grease remover, then wipe it off with a clean towel. Just be sure to label the bottle with its actual contents.

that are present onto a larger area and also further embedding those contaminants into the surface. If the surface isn't clean before you apply primer or paint, these materials will not adhere properly. Even oil from your fingers is enough to impact proper adhesion, so avoid touching the surface with your bare hands.

To obtain a clean surface, use wax and grease remover. These products are readily available at any paint supplier and are relatively inexpensive—which means there's no reason not to have them on hand in your shop. After using an air gun to blow away dust or dirt on the surface, apply the wax and grease remover with a clean cloth or paper towel, or spray it onto the surface. Wipe the surface dry with a clean, dry cloth or paper towel.

Using clean cloths is critical. Any old shop towel you pick up may have grease, brake fluid, or other contaminants, which will only add to the residue on your surface.

Fiberglass

For custom work or bodywork repair, you can easily learn to work with fiberglass, a material doesn't require specialized equipment. Obviously, fiberglass can be used to repair components made of the same material, but it can also be used as an alternative to welding in sheet metal patch panels (see the "Patch Panels" section in Chapter 7 for more on that process).

Fiberglass mat is commonly used when repairing holes or anywhere you need to build up bulk. Composed of short strands of glass fibers bound together, not woven, the mat is saturated with fiberglass resin, making it quite pliable and easy to form into complex shapes. As each layer of fiberglass mat is added, the laminate becomes thicker and stiffer.

Fiberglass cloth is more suitable to repairing cracks, breaks, or holes where there are few complex shapes. Since fiberglass cloth is made of woven glass thread, it is difficult to mold to curved shapes without wrinkling. To get the cloth to lie flat on a curved surface, several small cuts can be made in the cloth before the resin is applied. Fiberglass cloth is thinner than fiberglass mat, so avoid using cloth when your goal is to build up bulk in the repair area. However, a repair made with cloth will be stronger than a repaired area made with an equal thickness of mat, since the cloth contains a larger amount of glass.

Fiberglass mat and cloth is available in different widths, lengths, and weights for jobs of different size. For the beginner, working with smaller pieces of cloth or mat will be easier than trying to work with larger pieces.

Fiberglass resin bonds fiberglass mat or cloth. This resin is made from a mixture of two elements: a thick liquid and a small amount of hardener. The amount of hardener used varies, depending on the ambient air temperature and humidity, and the amount of working time you desire when working with the material. As the fiberglass resin cures, or "kicks," a chemical reaction occurs between the liquid resin and the hardener, resulting in the resin, mat, and cloth becoming solid—and very hot. Be sure to have adequate skin and eye protection when working with fiberglass. Also, work in an adequately ventilated area to vent the fumes given off by the curing fiberglass; these fumes can be intense and people with respiratory problems may experience a bad reaction to them. Once the fiberglass has cured, wear a nuisance mask and eye and skin protection any time you sand, drill, or cut this material.

To estimate how much resin you will need when making a repair, the first coat you apply will take approximately 1 pint of resin to saturate 1 square yard of cloth thoroughly, while you will need 1½ quarts of resin to saturate 1 square yard of mat thoroughly. After the first coat, each of the subsequent coats you apply will require only half as much resin.

When mixing and working with fiberglass, think "disposable," not cleanable, when choosing containers and mixing implements. Fiberglass resin can be mixed in disposable paint tray liners, picnic/party cups, empty gallon milk jugs, or nearly anything that is clean and can hold the liquid resin. Common paint stirrers work well to mix the resin and hardener, while disposable paintbrushes work well to spread the resin onto the cloth or mat. These disposable containers are cheaper to replace than the materials for cleaning them, so don't worry about saving them for later jobs.

However, your hands are not disposable, so be sure to cover them with disposable latex gloves. You should also have some acetone available for cleanup, in case you happen to get some resin on your hands or skin.

Plastic Body Filler

No matter how good you may be with a body hammer, if you have straightened any sheet metal or installed patch panels, you will probably need to apply at least a skim coat of body filler. True, there are some craftsmen who can finish metal on a vehicle so perfectly that they don't need filler. However, you probably aren't working at that level of expertise yet. Before applying any filler, take the time to consult an expert and verify that you are using compatible materials. You'll be much better off if you determine the appropriate filler product for your use before starting work.

Consider the material to which you're applying the body filler: sheet metal, galvanized steel, fiberglass, or aluminum. It's always better to do the work correctly the first time than have to do it a second (or third) time or have to live with results that leave a lot to be desired.

If you purchase your bodywork supplies at a dealer who sells to professionals, the person behind the counter most likely knows which products are best for your particular application. However, if you look for body filler at the local discount retailer, you may be hard-pressed to find someone who even knows how to use this product. While the label of most body fillers will indicate how they are used on bare metals, that information will probably not explain how to apply the product on your particular project.

Not all body fillers are created equal, as they are designed for specific applications. As with choosing paint materials, you should stick with one brand of fillers to eliminate compatibility problems.

Plastic body fillers have evolved greatly since they appeared on the market as an alternative to lead. Several different companies now make plastic body filler, and most offer a variety of products to choose from, depending on your application. Some fillers are designed for use over fiberglass, while others are designed for sheet metal; still others call for an undercoat of epoxy primer to increase adhesion or an application performed directly on bare metal. Like many primer products, some fillers smooth out rough bodywork, while others are used for finish coats. Put simply, not all body fillers are created equal or even to perform the same task. If you use the wrong type of filler, this will show soon after the vehicle is parked in the sun. And I doubt you plan on keeping your car parked in the garage forever.

PRODUCT	DESCRIPTION	CHARACTERISTICS	TYPICAL USES
Evercoat Everglass® FIB-622	Short strand, fiberglass reinforced body filler	High strength, high build, and waterproof	Repairing holes, rusted metal, body seams, and shattered fiberglass; used as the first filler over any welds
Evercoat Rage® Gold FIB-112	Pinhole-free body filler	Superior adhesion to galvanized steel and aluminum, high-grade resin reduces risk of staining	Filling low areas of bodywork on galvanized steel or aluminum surfaces; used as the second coat of filler over Everglass®
Evercoat Rage® Xtreme FIB-120	Pinhole-free body filler	Self-leveling, easy spreading, easily sands with 80-grit sandpaper	Filling low areas of bodywork; used to finish areas of Rage® Gold
Evercoat METALWORKS® Z-Grip FIB-282	Lightweight body filler	Excellent adhesion to galvanized steel, aluminum, and epoxy primers	Filling corrosion prone areas
Evercoat Metal Glaze® FIB-416	Polyester finishing and blending putty	Can be used over bare metal and all body fillers	Used in conjunction with other METALWORKS® body fillers and glazing putties to enhance their ease of working
Evercoat METALWORKS® Spot-Lite® FIB-445	Lightweight finishing putty	Excellent adhesion to galvanized steel, aluminum, and plastics	Final filling of galvanized steel, aluminum, and plastics

Most likely, you will need at least a skim coat of body filler whenever you straighten sheet metal that has been damaged in an accident. Evercoat is one of several companies that manufacture a complete line of body fillers for various applications. The chart found elsewhere in this chapter will assist you in determining which filler is correct for your particular application.

Nearly all body fillers require the same methods for application, but you should read the directions for the particular product to be sure. Typically, the surface to be filled is sanded down to bare metal before applying filler. Some fillers suggest that the surface be stripped of any paint and a coat of epoxy primer applied before starting with filler. Most auto body paint and supply stores can provide printed information that indicates the compatibility of their products.

Whether you're applying filler to bare metal or fiberglass, or to a primered surface, some amount of filler material is spread onto a mixing board or mixing sheet and then mixed *thoroughly* with a proportionate amount of hardener, using a flexible spreader. The amount of hardener needed depends on your shop conditions, such as the temperature and humidity. Practice is the best way to determine how much to use. As a start, though, add a proportionate amount of hardener to the filler (i.e., a quarter tube of hardener to a quarter of the container of filler). Use too little hardener and it will not set up properly, while too much hardener will set up right on your mixing board. Don't be surprised if it takes the entire project before you get the amounts right. If it gets a little too cool as you mix it, speed the curing process slightly by placing a portable heater or heat lamp nearby. If the filler begins to "kick" before you have it spread out, scrape it off the mixing board and throw it away: you won't be able to spread it properly.

Most body fillers use a hardener that is distinctly different in color than the filler itself: this makes it easy to tell when the two are mixed thoroughly. When the mix is the same color throughout, it is well mixed; if there are streaks of color, keep on mixing. Once the filler and the hardener are mixed thoroughly (i.e., the material is all one color), scoop some filler onto a flexible spreader and spread the filler on the target area, then make a couple of light passes with an empty spreader to even out the filler.

For best results, don't apply body filler more than 1/8 inch thick total. If you need more than this, try to metalwork the area being repaired slightly more before applying any filler. If hammer and dolly work isn't feasible, and the area to be filled is deeper than 1/8 inch, use two applications of filler rather than attempting to fill it all at one time. Like most auto body repair products, filler cures as its various chemical components react and escape from the remaining material. Too thick an application will often cure on the outside before the chemical reaction takes place on the inside, trapping uncured material inside the repair. When this happens, the repair won't be durable and will ultimately show up in the finished paint job.

Some older types of filler require initial smoothing, with a cheese-grater type file, while most newer products can be smoothed initially with 80-grit sandpaper. Check with the person behind the counter where you purchase your products to determine the best method for smoothing. If you are using any type of filler that requires a cheese grater, initial smoothing should take place right before the filler cures completely. Watch the edges of the filler to get a feel for whether it has cured enough. If the filler starts breaking away at the edges, or if the sandpaper starts loading up, the filler has not cured sufficiently.

While it's hard to say what the correct time for curing will be, a little practice will reveal how long you need to wait. Knock off the high spots before the filler gets rock-hard, but don't try this too soon or you'll likely gouge out more material than desired. As you begin working the filler, sand the entire filled area first with 80- or 100-grit sandpaper, then switch to 200- or 240-grit to blend the filler into the surrounding area. Once you're finished sanding with 240-grit, you will have a good idea if you need more filler before you apply primer.

When you finish sanding, blow all of the dust away with an air nozzle. If there are still low spots, rough up the area lightly with the previous grit of sandpaper, then mix an appropriate amount of body filler and apply as before. Work the second and successive layers of filler (if required) just as the first, until all low areas are filled.

Sandpaper

Before applying sealer and paint, work the area over with sandpaper: no need to start sealing too soon. You'll use lots of sandpaper before the project is finished, but damaged body panels should be *straightened* long before finishing the sanding process. Use sandpaper for smoothing thin coats of body filler, scuffing a primed surface prior to applying additional coats of primer or sealer, and for wet sanding clear coats after applying paint.

Avoid wet sanding until you know what you're doing and you have the correct material. Only use sandpaper designed for wet sanding. Using sandpaper that isn't designed for this will simply fall apart when it gets wet.

Wet sanding should only be used after the vehicle has been painted. Extremely fine (1,000-grit or finer) sandpaper is moved in a circular motion, with light pressure, after being dipped in a water bucket or by spraying water onto the surface. The wet sanding process removes the orange-peel effect from the paint, while the water helps float away the paint being removed, instead of simply rubbing it back into the surface.

On some high-dollar, custom-built vehicles, the body man may use a wet sanding technique prior to paint in order to get the smoothest surface possible. For repairs to your daily driver, this is probably overkill and as such is a wasted effort. Pouring water on a piece of bare sheet metal or into an area of body filler is not a good approach. Unless you are highly skilled, this can lead to more problems as you try your hand at bodywork.

In summary, since most of your work will involve sanding dry, grab a dust mask and a sanding block. For removing paint and getting down to bare metal, a 36- or 50-grit disc on an electric or pneumatic sander works best if you are working on a localized repair. Complete paint removal on entire panels calls for chemical stripping or a media-blast approach. As mentioned above, initial shaping of body filler works best when you use 80- or 100-grit sandpaper over the entire filled area, then switch to 200- or 240-grit sandpaper to blend the filler into the surrounding areas. Finally, sand the entire area you're going to repaint after repair with 400-grit sandpaper.

Seam Sealer

Seam sealer is much like caulking for automobiles. Although it is available in forms that can be brushed on, it is typically dispensed from a tube. As its name would imply, it is used for sealing seams in sheet metal from moisture or dirt that would eventually allow the formation of rust. Common areas of use include floor panels and trunk areas where the floor meets the inner fender or wheelhouse. Any location prone to collecting and trapping moisture will be a good candidate for seam sealer, as its application is much easier and less expensive than replacing rusty sheet metal. Most seam sealer products can be applied directly to bare sheet metal or over primered surfaces, but they are usually applied before painting.

Panel-Bonding Adhesives

One of the biggest recent innovations in automotive bodywork is the development and use of panel-bonding adhesives. As automotive manufacturers have worked to decrease the overall weight of their vehicles, they have begun using body components made of composites, rather than steel. Bonding adhesives were developed to handle composite materials, which cannot be welded using the same methods as those used for welding steel. Taking a good thing further, panel-bonding adhesives are now available for use with steel panels.

Many companies produce panel-bonding adhesives, with different products on the market available to address different situations. Be sure to read the package labels closely to ensure that you purchase the correct product for your application. You can find products for assembling rigid composites and flexible products. These are used in roughly the same way, but you should find the correct materials to achieve the best results for your repair work.

Most panel-bonding adhesives are made of a two-part epoxy. Improper mixing is a common source of failure for any type of two-part epoxy, so manufacturers have developed a system that mixes the two parts as they are used, rather than relying on the user to measure and mix thoroughly. Packaged in a tube, the epoxy components work like the caulking used for sealing around household windows or bathtubs. Each component is inserted into a specialized application tool, similar to a caulking gun. After removing air from both tubes, a mixing tube is attached to the tip of the application tool. As you squeeze the trigger, both components are blended as they travel through the mixing tube. Typically, the adhesive is applied to both surfaces being attached. The work pieces are then positioned and clamped into place. Most panels are cured in less than 24 hours, but heat lamps or other controlled applications of heat speed up the process considerably.

While panel-bonding adhesives will not completely eliminate the need for welding steel when doing bodywork, they have minimized welding substantially in both the auto manufacturing and collision repair industries. Not only is panel bonding a timesaver: it's been found to be just as strong and durable as welded panels when involved in a collision. This material also eliminates the risk of panels becoming warped when subjected to significant heat through conventional methods of welding: they are not prone to catching fire. The downside of this type of repair is the application tool's cost, but, in a collision repair shop, it will quickly pay for itself in reduced labor costs. However, a hobbyist may find the tool too expensive for making one-time repairs.

SPRAY APPLICATIONS

Bodywork doesn't require spray application, which means that you don't need an air compressor to straighten your recently dented fender. If you live in the desert, where there is virtually no humidity, and you are comfortable with a hammer and dolly, you can metal-finish your ride and be done. However, if you feel less comfortable working with metal and your climate includes snow, salt, and rain, repainting the repaired area is recommended.

Use an air compressor to apply the various substrates that fall between straightening and painting. Substrates are the various fillers and primers applied to the surface material before actually applying paint. These layers have just as much impact on the quality of the final paint job as the paint itself.

Etching or Epoxy Primer

Paint applied with no primer after finishing bodywork will most likely peel off in large sections. Many American automobiles manufactured in the late 1980s and early 1990s are common examples of this effect: these vehicles were primered before paint was applied, but the primer was not compatible with the surface. Vehicles from this era saw paint peeling off in sheets, exposing the surface below to the weather.

The main purpose for primer is to promote adhesion between the surface being repaired and the subsequent top coats, whether body filler or paint. No one universal primer product will adequately prepare every surface for paint. Choose primer for the material that it is intended to cover. Fiberglass calls for different primer than aluminum, which requires different primer than galvanized steel. Some materials can be primed with regular primer, while others are better suited for epoxy primer.

Two main reasons for using epoxy primer are its superior corrosion protection and excellent adhesion qualities, yet epoxy primer cannot be used for every application. Consult your local paint jobber for recommendations on the best primer for your particular needs. Any time a sheet metal panel is stripped (whether chemically or mechanically) to bare metal, it should be cleaned and coated with etching or epoxy primer as soon as possible, to avoid the formation of surface rust. Most body fillers can be applied over etching or epoxy primer, so there will be no reason to go back to bare metal during the repair process.

Polyester Spray Body Filler

A relatively new primer product, sprayable body filler can be used over bare metal, aluminum, fiberglass, and most other body fillers. Since this is a thicker filler type

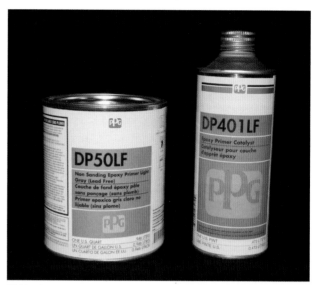

PPG's DP-series of epoxy primer is an excellent self-etching primer that can be used directly on bare metal to provide corrosion protection. It also increases the adhesion qualities of body fillers and other primers. As a two-part epoxy, it consists of the actual primer and a hardener that must be mixed according to a specific mixing ratio before use. It can also be mixed in a different, yet specific ratio for use as a sealer prior to applying color coats.

than most primers or paints, it will require a spray gun nozzle tip of 2.2 or larger for application. Apply three or four light coats, then block-sand with 120-grit sandpaper and apply a guide coat (dusting) of a contrasting color spray enamel. Next, block-sand the guide coat with 180-grit sandpaper, apply another guide coat, and block-sand again with 220-grit sandpaper.

Primer-Surfacer

Offering a high solids content, primer-surfacers (also known as high build primer) are used to cover slight imperfections such as sanding scratches. These products should not be confused with or used as a filler, as they are not intended to fill more than slight scratches. Primer-surfacer is an undercoat product designed to be sanded smooth.

After applying primer-surfacer, it is usually block-sanded smooth with 320-grit sandpaper. Apply a second coat, allow this to dry, apply a guide coat of a contrasting color of spray-can enamel, and then block-sand with 400-grit paper and finish with 500-grit sandpaper until all of the guide coat has been removed.

Sealers

To prevent the solvent from top coats seeping into the various undercoats, apply a sealer. This will add maximum adhesion capabilities and ensure uniform color

Omni is a budget-minded series of paint and refinish products made by PPG. Shown here is their primer-surfacer that is used to fill sanding scratches in sheet metal or body filler. Known as a high fill primer, it still doesn't take the place of body filler. A high percentage of primer-surfacer is sanded off in the block sanding process of perfecting the body prior to paint application.

match. Sealers should also be used whenever applying new paint over a factory finish that has been baked on at temperatures around 450 degrees Fahrenheit. With the durability and hardness of these factory finishes, it is difficult for new paint to penetrate the surface and establish proper adhesion. If new paint is applied without first scuffing (using 180- to 220-grit sandpaper) and sealing the surface, new paint will most likely flake or even peel off in sheets.

MASKING SUPPLIES

Although HVLP spray guns minimize the amount of overspray when used for spraying primer or paint, you still need to mask off areas where you don't want your spray to reach. Even though proper masking takes a fair amount of time, it takes less time than cleaning overspray from unwanted areas.

Masking Tape

Most everyone is familiar with ordinary hardware- or household-grade masking tape, but don't use this kind of tape when spraying automotive primers and paint products. Ordinary household masking tape hasn't been treated to withstand the potent solvents used in automotive paint. Additionally, adhesives used in ordinary masking tape are not designed to break loose

easily from surfaces and can remain on painted bodies after the bulk of material has been pulled off. Lingering traces of tape and adhesive residue might require use of a mild solvent for complete removal, a chore that could threaten the finish or new paint applied next to it. Whether your job consists of a very small paint touchup or complete paint job, automotive paint masking tape is the only product designed for such use. Using any other type of inexpensive alternative is just asking for problems and aggravation.

Automotive-grade masking tape is available in sizes ranging from ⅛ inch up to 2 inches wide. You will likely use ¾-inch masking tape for most purposes, but having a couple of extra sizes will make your masking work easier. It is much simpler to place a few strips of 2-inch-wide masking tape over a headlight than to maneuver a sheet of masking paper over that same relatively small area.

Masking Paper

Rolls of quality automotive paint masking paper are available at auto body paint supply stores in widths ranging from 4 inches up to 3 feet. Masking paper is chemically treated to prevent paint or solvent from penetrating through it. You will seldom find professional auto painters using anything but treated masking paper for any masking job. Although newspaper material may seem inexpensive and appropriate for paint masking chores, it is porous and can let paint seep through to mar the surface finishes underneath. Anyone who uses masking paper will tell you that a masking paper dispenser is worth the extra money it costs, as it makes masking the vehicle much easier and faster.

Fine Line Tape

For masking along trim or moldings that cannot be removed prior to priming or painting, use ⅛-inch 3M Fine Line tape. It is easy to use as a primary masking edge along trim and molding edges, as it is very maneuverable, and will adhere securely around curves without bending or folding. After placing the Fine Line tape at the edge of whatever is being masked, ¾-inch masking tape can be attached to the Fine Line tape without laying it right at the edge of the masked area.

Chapter 3
Developing a Repair Strategy

Okay, it actually happened. You, your spouse, son, or daughter got into a minor fender bender. The damage doesn't look extensive. For reasons that have already been discussed, you don't want to turn it in to your insurance, but you also don't want to pay what the body shop quotes for repairing the damage. Now is the time to step up to the plate and fix it yourself. However, before you pick up a hammer and dolly, you need to assess the damage and develop a repair strategy. Having a plan will play a major part in getting the vehicle repaired and back on the road quickly.

BODY/CHASSIS CONSTRUCTION TYPES

During the 100-plus years of automobile manufacture, the basic construction has changed substantially. For the most part, those changes have typically been to facilitate improvements of some sort. Our vehicles have evolved from a body being mounted on a frame, to unibody construction (with no frame), to a body that has the framework concealed within the floor panel. Prior to fully assessing the damage (and the repair philosophy) of any vehicle, we must fully understand how the vehicle in question is designed to go back together.

A couple of frames from vehicles that use body-on-frame construction; note that the frame in the background is upside-down. The profile of these frames is raised on both ends, allowing the vehicle to sit lower. The frame in the foreground has supports mounted outboard of the frame rails to mount the body, while the frame in the background does not. Also note that the frame in the front uses an "X"-type crossmember to strengthen the frame.

Full Frame Construction

Nearly all passenger vehicles manufactured in the United States, up to and including the early 1960s, were built with a sheet metal body bolted to a heavy steel framework. Most of these vehicle frames consisted of a pair of frame rails tied together by crossmembers. The frame rails run front-to-back, are roughly parallel to each other, and are typically closer to the outer edges of the body. Typically, there are three or four crossmembers in a vehicle, but that number will vary according to make and model. Still, one crossmember is usually located near the front of the frame, one at the back, with another crossmember located near the middle of the vehicle, and often used in conjunction with supporting the engine and/or transmission. Over the years, the profile and layout of the frame rails have changed to better fit the body style of the vehicle to which it is mounted.

This full-frame construction has many advantages over other types of construction. Within any one company's line of vehicles, many body styles use the same frame. For instance, a stock 1934 Ford frame could be used for a coupe, a roadster, a sedan, or a light-duty pickup truck. This is also true for vehicles manufactured up to the 1960s; although there were more models to choose from in this period, fewer frames types were used. All of the General Motors A-body vehicles utilize the same frame, regardless of their use of branded (Chevrolet, Pontiac, Oldsmobile, or Buick) sheet metal.

This early 1930s Hudson Terraplane sedan features full-frame construction. A front crossmember mounts the front axle and spring. An aftermarket K-member replaces the stock transmission crossmember.

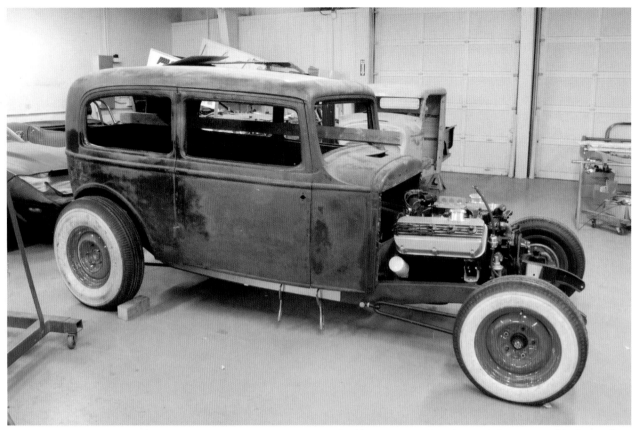

The same chassis with the body bolted onto the frame. Mounting bolts pass through the floorpan and thread into threaded holes in the top of the frame rails.

The suspension assembly (shocks, springs, axles, wheels, and tires) attaches to the frame, with none of these items attaching to the body. This makes disassembly and reassembly straightforward. There was a time when it was not uncommon to find a wrecked 1932 Ford frame and drivetrain in a salvage yard for an affordable price. With the help of a couple of friends on a Saturday afternoon, an older, lightweight, cheaper Model A Ford body could be installed in time to pick up a date for Saturday night or go racing on Sunday.

More importantly for the context of this book, the body being separate from the frame makes some bodywork tasks easier. To strip paint, the body could be removed from the frame and suspension and be taken to a media blaster or chemical stripper. This eliminates the chances of inflicting unintentional damage to the frame or suspension. However, even though some bodywork can be done while the body is off the frame, significant surgery on the body (such as modifying or replacing sheet metal panels and/or performing substantial welding) requires that it be bolted securely to the frame. This will help eliminate warping and other problems.

Unibody Construction (No Frame)

During the 1960s, American passenger cars were built using unibody construction. In other words, there was no longer a full structural frame beneath the vehicle. Instead, a cradle-type framework was bolted or welded to the bottom of the floorpan and sometimes to the lower portion of the firewall. This cradle looks similar to the front portion of a conventional frame, serving to mount the engine and transmission. The rear suspension attaches to rear subrails that are bolted or welded to the underside of the floorpan. The rear axle housing is connected to the subrails via shocks and springs.

Whether the front cradle and rear subrails are welded or bolted to the underside of the body, they are the link between the suspension and the body sheet metal. Because of this, many vehicles of this type can tear themselves apart due to forces of torque and traction. While this may not be a problem in a low-power commuter car, a vehicle with some power under the hood will begin twisting due to torque. On a full-frame vehicle, the frame is typically sturdy enough to absorb this force—but sheet metal isn't. As the torque continues, it effectively pulls the rear subrails away from the sheet metal body. This area of the vehicle often becomes a target for rust, making the matter worse.

The old cliché about a house being only as good as its foundation can also apply to a vehicle. While a stock-bodied vehicle of unibody construction may last a long time if it's never pushed to the limit, that same vehicle being driven—shall we say, "enthusiastically"—eventually faces fatigue where the suspension bolts to the floorpan.

Installing subframe connectors is one method for strengthening the body. These are usually constructed from rectangular steel tubing and attach to the bottom of the vehicle's floor pan between the front cradle and the rear subrails. The takeaway from this discussion about unibody construction is that a quick glance at a vehicle may suggest that a floor pan repair may just call for some quick work with a MIG welder to install a flat piece of sheet metal. In reality, however, such repair may require installing a new subrail and possibly some suspension work.

Pickup/SUV Construction

While many of the smaller SUVs on today's market use a unibody style of construction, full-size SUVs and pickup trucks continue to use a full-frame type construction. Although pickup trucks are certainly more popular now than they have ever been for hauling the family, they are still designed to haul bulkier payloads. For this reason, they still rely on a ladder-type frame with two frame rails that are mostly parallel to each other, along with a series of crossmembers that tie the two together. This simple structure will make the vehicle rigid, but it can also be fit with stiffer or softer suspensions to dial in the desired load range and comfort level.

Since the chassis and body are ultimately two separate components, full-size SUV and pickup truck chassis are often the basis for some interesting vehicles. Older vehicle bodies are often placed on a newer four-wheel drive chassis. Although four-wheel drive is very common now, it was not available on production vehicles (other than Willys Jeeps) until

Just slightly outboard of the shiny exhaust is the subframe connector that links the front cradle to the rear subrails.

This frame is for a 1955 Chevrolet pickup, yet it is very similar in basic design to a contemporary pickup chassis. A pair of frame rails run front to back and mostly parallel to each other. These are tied together by multiple crossmembers. This type of chassis design is often referred to as a ladder design.

the late 1950s. In other words, this type of chassis allows for outfitting a vintage pickup with four-wheel drive, if that is your desire.

BODY CONSTRUCTION

Just as chassis construction has evolved, so has the automobile's body design. Not only do the bodies of new vehicles look different than those of new vehicles, they are made differently as well. In the 1930s, many American-made automobile bodies were pieces of sheet metal nailed to pieces of wood and bolted together. As you might imagine, with age, the wood rotted, the nails fell out, and nothing was left to support the sheet metal, which simply rusted away. This, perhaps, is one of the main reasons that so many hot rods built by service-men returning from World War II were based on Ford bodies. These bodies were formed pieces of sheet metal bolted together and supported by a wooden superstruc-ture, a subtle but important difference in automotive history. Sure, the wood would rot when the vehicle was

abandoned, but the formed sheet metal was more likely to retain its shape and could still be usable with the addi-tion of a new wood kit.

During the 1940s and 1950s, American automakers were able to stamp larger pieces of sheet metal into more complex shapes. Thicker sheet metal and complex shapes allowed the bodies and components to become more freestanding, eliminating the need for a wooden superstructure.

In the 1980s and 1990s, fuel mileage became a focal point among auto manufacturers, so lighter body construction became important. This led to the use of composite materials for body construction, as well as for fenders and bumpers.

Sheet Metal

While sheet metal can be stamped into almost any shape, one piece alone cannot be stamped into an entire automobile body. Typically, several body com-ponents are stamped into shape, trimmed, and then

This truck cab has received some damage to the left lower corner in some past accident; also note some shoddy repair. The damage was evident even before the body was stripped, but is fully apparent now that some of the body filler and primer have been removed. The replacement panel was not welded in squarely. An entire new back panel is now available and will be welded in to correct this inferior repair.

bolted or welded together. The largest single component is the actual body, which is comprised of the floor, firewall, rear quarter panels, and roof. These pieces are welded together, usually with some amount of lead filler used at the joints to make the body appear to be one large piece of sheet metal, in reality a design that is not possible or feasible. The vehicle's doors, trunk (deck lid), front fenders, and hood are bolted onto this body assembly.

In days gone by, if the rear quarter panel was damaged beyond what could be repaired with hammer and dolly work and some body filler, the vehicle was totaled. Or you could purchase a similar vehicle out of a salvage yard and cut and weld portions of the two bodies back together, as required. However, as these sheet metal bodies are made up of components, many of these components are now being reproduced, making it easier to resurrect these often rusted-out hulks.

Fiberglass and Composites

While fiberglass has been used in construction of production vehicles since 1954 (in the Chevrolet Corvette), its primary automotive use has been for repair and/or customization. However, auto manufacturers have started using various composites more commonly in their designs. These composites are undoubtedly less expensive to produce and lighter, making it easier for manufacturers to meet their fuel mileage requirements. While these panels are referred to as "dent-resistant," they will often break upon impact. Which is less offensive: a dented sheet metal panel or a hole in a composite panel? Fortunately, they are both repairable.

MODULAR BODY CONSTRUCTION

With the advent of composite auto body panels came an additional, albeit separate, superstructure beneath them. This paved the way for replacing individual components of a body assembly without smoothing and covering the welds with lead. Having the ability to install individual panels during the manufacturing process, as well as quickly replacing them during collision repair, led to the research and development of body panel adhesives.

Glued-On Body Panels

Automotive manufacturing companies have been using body panel adhesives on composite panels since their inception, but they have also begun using them on sheet metal in some instances as well. Eliminating the welding process no doubt reduces labor costs, as proper welding takes time. It also minimizes the risk of fire, which can be very expensive in a manufacturing environment. Although MIG welding is easy to learn, body-panel adhesives are probably more generally applicable and easier to use.

RADIATOR CORE SUPPORT

Regardless of the body/chassis construction type, in nearly all front-engine models, a radiator core support is used up front. While the frame provides support from front to back, the core support that fits perpendicular to the frame provides a lateral support for mounting fenders, the radiator, and other items. The significance of this is that, if the core support is damaged or in any way falls out of position, the front fenders are not going to mount and/or align properly with the vehicle's body.

ASSESSING THE DAMAGE

Now that we have discussed the necessary tools and materials required to perform basic bodywork repair, it is time to look at the project at hand. There may be some portions of the damaged vehicle that can be repaired, while others may be beyond repair. What is

The radiator core support forms a basic rectangular frame that mounts the radiator to the frame, but also provides upper and lower mounting points for the fronts of the fenders. It also serves as mounting points for headlights, grille on the front side, as well as various mechanical pieces on the engine side. If this support has been crunched, as the one in this early 1990s GMC S15, it must be replaced in order to reassemble this vehicle.

Damage to this S15 is limited to the area in front of the firewall. Still, in most cases, it would have been totaled out by an insurance company. Of course, financial issues often make repairing the vehicle the practical course of action, rather than reporting an accident to the insurance company. Obvious items that need to be replaced are the hood, right front fender, grille, gravel pan (AKA valance), front bumper, and right headlight. Other not-so-obvious items that must be addressed are the radiator, a/c system, electrical issues, hood latch, and any mechanical issues that may have gone unnoticed.

important as you assess the damage is to note which portions can be repaired successfully and which parts require replacement.

Unless you are sure that the damage is limited to exterior sheet metal, you might want to take the damaged vehicle to a reputable body shop for an estimate, if you have not done so already. This will serve you in a couple of ways, and possibly more if you are completely new to auto repair and will need to purchase tools to make the repair.

First, and most importantly, an experienced estimator will know how to look for hidden damage and will often list the parts that need to be replaced. This will give you a better idea of the scope of needed repairs. Secondly, the quote will indeed tell you how much the body shop will charge to complete the repair. If the repair is significant and labor intensive, you will quickly realize that your labor rate is much more affordable than theirs, providing you have the time.

If a hammer and dolly, a gallon of plastic body filler, some sandpaper, and a quart of paint will be your only expenses, you can do the work for less money than what you would pay the body shop. Additionally, if you want to purchase an air compressor and/or other tools anyway, using them for this repair might be justifiable. Still, such tools are expensive. All things considered, if you can get the tools you want and fix the car fixed for the same amount of money . . . I can give you the idea, but you still have to sell the idea to the holder of the purse strings.

If/when you take your damaged vehicle to an auto body repair shop, a very common question from the service writer will be "Is your insurance paying for this or are you?" Your answer doesn't mean that they will automatically jack up the price just because the insurance company is paying for it, but this will have an impact on how the repair is made—and therefore can affect the bottom line. Since insurance companies also usually pay for loaner cars while yours is in the shop, they want to get your vehicle back to you as soon as possible.

This all boils down the fact that many sheet metal panels, which could be repaired by a competent body man, are instead just replaced in the interest of time. These replacement parts are more expensive to purchase, but they require less labor to refinish. Depending on the particular vehicle, the parts may be much more expensive than the necessary labor. Additionally, disassembly and reassembly labor must be factored into the quote. It is quite conceivable that two quotes for the same damaged vehicle (one to replace, one to repair) could be substantially different.

What Can be Repaired?

Of course, we know that you are going to take on this repair yourself and all of the money spent on it is coming straight out of your pocket. Since your labor rate is negligible at this point, you should straighten, smooth, and refinish every damaged piece that you can, rather than replace it.

In body shops that do insurance work, many brackets, actuator levers, and other hidden parts that are damaged slightly are replaced rather than repaired. The logic is that the customer turns the repair over to the insurance company so that the repairs will be made correctly and completely. That's why we all pay for insurance, so that, when something bad does happen,

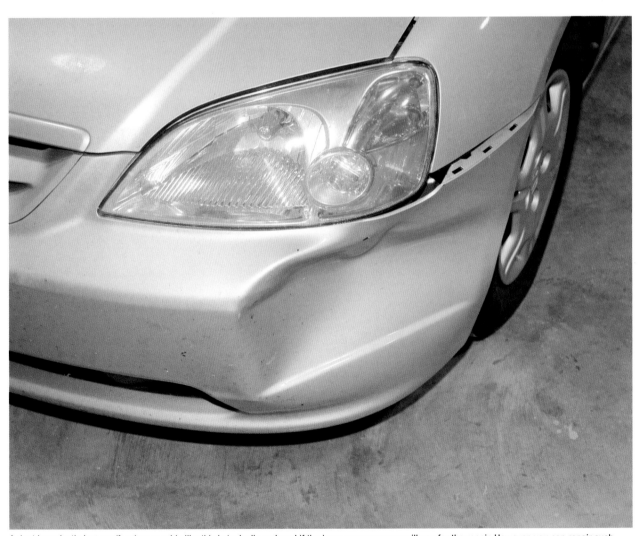

A dent in a plastic bumper/fascia assembly like this is typically replaced if the insurance company will pay for the repair. However, you can repair such damage if you are completing the repairs yourself. By using a heat gun (something more substantial than a hair dryer), the panel can be heated to the point of being more pliable and pushed back out to close to its original shape. It can then be left as-is for a no-cost repair, or a skim coat of filler can be applied, sanded, and repainted.

Severe damage to a passenger car's rear quarter panel is often reason enough to total the vehicle. If the vehicle is not totaled, the repair often consists of cutting out the affected panel and welding in a replacement. On this Ford Explorer, however, damage was minimal, requiring only some minor bodywork, priming, and block sanding. The affected area was masked off and repainted later in the day.

This pickup truck tailgate had significant damage, so it was replaced rather than repaired. Since this repair was being turned over to the owner's insurance company, the latch mechanism, linkage, and brackets were replaced as well to make sure that the tailgate would operate correctly. If you were making the repair yourself, you could save some money by spending a little bit of time straightening these components.

The old latch mechanism is at left, with the replacement at right. If you look closely, you will see that the brass-colored rod is bent slightly on the original latch. Using this damaged latch could make it difficult to open the tailgate. The linkage rods and brackets, however, could be straightened with little or no adverse effects. None of the damaged components will be visible once reinstalled, except for the outer portion of the latch, which is not damaged on the outside.

the bad goes away, and it's as if nothing happened. But some of these brackets could be straightened, if desired. You're not going to see these particular parts inside the hood, door, or deck lid anyway, so you shouldn't care if some paint is chipped a little. And, as long as the piece functions properly, you can live with it, right? That's where you have to decide what can be repaired. A reputable body shop will err toward customer satisfaction because their reputation is at stake. When you are repairing your vehicle, your wallet is the most vulnerable part of the equation.

What Must be Replaced?

Given enough time, nearly any dented automotive sheet metal can be straightened. However, if any of those panels has a crease pressed into it as the result of an accident, you should probably consider replacing the affected panel, as the crease will be very difficult to remove. Small rips or tears in sheet metal panels can be repaired by welding the metal back together, even if this requires welding in a patch panel.

Many newer vehicles have plastic panels instead of or around the traditional bumper areas at the front or rear of the vehicle. Some of these panels are made of rigid plastic that will break on impact. These can be repaired, assuming that the pieces are all there and can be clamped together back in the correct shape. If significant portions of the panel are missing, or they're damaged to the point that you have no way to clamp them back into the correct shape, you may save time by simply purchasing a replacement part. Other plastic panels are more flexible and designed to be less likely to break. However, this softer plastic will distort if pushed beyond its resilient state. A simple dent

Besides the drivetrain components, which suffered considerable damage, the front fender, bumper/fascia assembly, and headlight all required replacement on this Buick. A portion of the fender was actually torn away and the plastic bumper/fascia assembly was distorted beyond its resilient state, making replacement rather than repair essential. The time spent trying to repair this damage simply exceeds the cost of panel replacement.

created by a single point of contact can be fixed, while multiple forces from different directions will most likely distort the panel beyond reasonable repair.

Analysis of Repair vs. Replacement

While determining your plan of attack for repairs, you should realistically consider the time required versus the time available, the cost of the necessary materials, and the overall quality of the repair that is your goal. Each individual places greater or lesser importance on each factor, and there is no one answer for the best approach that satisfies them all in every case. The answer depends (in part) on the vehicle being repaired and the situation at the time. However, once you've decide how best to make the repair, second-guessing your decision will impede your progress toward making the repair—and you won't learn how to do anything.

Time

For any activity, available time is probably the single largest deterrent for the do-it-yourselfer. Automotive repair is no different. Assuming that the damage is purely cosmetic and the vehicle is still drivable, you have more time available than if the vehicle is damaged beyond operability. Can the repairs be broken down into smaller steps, performing one or two steps at a time over a weekend? Even if it takes a month of weekends, or three, if you can complete the job yourself on this schedule, you will save yourself some labor fees. If you can't actually repair the affected panels according to this time frame, can your replace the damaged parts and get them primed and painted within your time constraints?

Especially if you are a beginner, everything will probably take longer than you want to complete the work. With this in mind, build extra time into your plans for refinishing replacement parts. If you have a critical deadline for having the repair completed, such as a son or daughter who needs their car repaired before heading back to college, you may need to replace the panels with the most damage and repair only the ones with minor damage.

Materials

If you are not tied to a deadline or are otherwise constricted by time, you can purchase the required body hammers, dollies, and body filler for less than the price of a replacement fender. If there are multiple panels that require repair or replacement, the cash investment in tools spreads itself out over the entire repair. It still costs you whatever you spend, but if, after finishing the repair, you have more tools in your toolbox and the experience to use them, you will be better off. At least you will be better equipped to handle the situation should something similar occur again. Remember that, if you have young drivers in the house, you may have more opportunities to practice your bodywork skills.

Overall Refinish Quality

Are you repairing the vehicle that your teenage son or daughter is learning to drive or is it the one that your spouse drives? If the repair to be completed has you wondering if you are capable, ask yourself, "How good does it have to be?" If you purchased a relatively cheap vehicle with more than a few minor dents and dings for your teenager to drive, the repair doesn't need to be on par with what would be required on a brand-new vehicle. Yes, you still want to fix it and make it look good, but in this situation you should probably lean toward repairing rather than replacing panels.

On the other hand, if the vehicle is in decent condition (beyond the recently smashed fender), replacing said fender or other panel could save you time. And the time you save could then be used for high-quality detailing, which will go a long way toward making the vehicle look like new again.

DETERMINING THE PARTS YOU NEED

Whether the recently damaged vehicle is being repaired at a professional collision repair shop or by you in your garage or driveway, the repair process starts with an estimate. This is where the body shop estimator and insurance adjuster make it or break it for their respective employers. Their task is to inspect the damaged vehicle thoroughly, to determine which parts must be replaced versus which parts can be repaired. While they are making this calculation, they are compiling a complete list of parts to be replaced, repaired, and/or refinished. The more thorough the list, the more accurate their estimate.

To complete the repair in a timely and efficient manner, you will need to perform your own estimate. Grab a clipboard with a pad of paper and a pen. While estimators have experience in knowing how vehicles come apart and go back together, they will know how to look for hidden damage. You might not know what to look for, but you have as much time as necessary to remove portions of the damaged parts to see what damage lies beneath. The estimator relies on experience to recognize what else may have been damaged.

Although further disassembly may reveal additional damage, you should begin collecting all of the parts you think you will need as soon as possible. You may need to store some of these parts for a while, so your decision should be based on your particular circumstances: should you buy now and store the parts until they are needed, or wait until you are ready to work on that specific part or section of the vehicle? For example, you'll be amazed how much space a fender or hood can take up when not attached. Availability is another factor in your decision: depending on the parts that you need and where you intend to get them, they may be readily available from your supplier, or they may be hard to find. If the metric left-handed wing nut widget that you need is on back order, your repair/reassembly process may grind to a halt while you are waiting for the part or tool.

New Parts

You can find replacement panels from a variety of sources suppliers; the key differences will come down to pricing and quality. Ideally, the parts that you need will be affordable and available new. New parts usually come from one of two sources: the original manufacturer (or licensed parts supplier), or a manufacturer of reproduction parts. Parts may be sold as from the original equipment manufacturer (OEM), but they may actually be new-old-stock (NOS), leftover parts that are no longer available as new from the dealer. Since they may be "rare" because they are no longer manufactured by the OEM supplier, NOS parts may have a higher price tag than parts that are still being produced. Beware, though of reproduction parts, which can be built by anyone: the quality of these varies from one manufacturer to another.

Your dealer's body shop will use genuine replacement panels from your vehicle's manufacturer if they are hired to make the repair. Such replacement panels will be made of brand-new sheet metal, with the original mounting holes, light recesses, and contours. As you might expect, these are the most expensive to purchase, although their higher quality fit may save time and trouble.

OEM or NOS

New parts are usually as close as the parts department of your local car dealership. While some parts may not be in stock, be sure to ask about estimated delivery time before ordering what you need. In addition to having the right parts, the parts counter staff usually has access to assembly drawings, which can be helpful. They may not let you print a copy of the drawings you need, but parts counter staff will usually let you go over the drawings. This should give you some insight when it comes to looking for any additional parts that you may need to replace.

Another benefit of working with an automotive dealer is that you can return most parts if you realize you don't actually need them (as long as you haven't modified them). If you can, hang on to your receipt and the packaging for possible returns. Even though you may be charged a restocking fee, at least you'll get some of your money back—which is more than you can say if you hang on to a part you really don't need.

New parts are preferable, in most cases, especially for parts made of sheet metal, such as fenders, doors, hoods, and deck lids. These new pieces are usually already primed, so you'll spend less time refinishing. Additionally, new parts should be free of rust or other blemishes. And you can expect them to fit correctly with your existing components, since any necessary mounting holes should already be in place.

Reproduction Parts

Reproduction parts are only as good as the aftermarket manufacturer wishes to make them. While there is no governing body that regulates the manufacture of reproductions (which means you should never take quality for granted), several companies manufacture very good replacement parts. Any problems with proper fit are usually not noticeable until after you've purchased the part and tried to install it, at which point you discover the poor fit. On the other hand, some replacement panels can be superior to the ones dealers carry. It pays to ask around before you buy. A part's cost is not always a good indication of its quality, either, so do some research before you plunk down your money on reproduction parts.

Although the actual wording will vary from one OEM to another, parts that are approved or officially licensed by the OEM will be displayed prominently in the catalog and packaging of their respective manufacturers. For example, parts from Goodmark Industries that Chrysler approves are labeled as Mopar Authentic Restoration Product. General Motors and Ford have similar labels for parts made by aftermarket sources that meet their approval.

When shopping for replacement panels, you will need to verify exactly how much metal you must replace prior to buying, as several similar panels may be available for the same vehicle. Do you need a panel that replaces only the wheel opening contours, all the way up to the top ridge of the rear quarter, or all the way to the trunk opening?

This particular full quarter covers all of the side and also wraps over to the edge of the trunk opening and the bottom of the sail panel, making for a pretty complete rear quarter repair on this early Mustang.

Sheet metal parts from some reproduction companies are not primed, so they may have some surface rust that you must remove before installation. Some of these panels fit better than others, which makes it necessary to elongate mounting holes in order to get the panels to align properly. Also, some panels can be wavy, requiring additional block sanding prior to the application of paint.

Used Parts

Used parts may be the best option for your repair, depending on the extent of the damage suffered, the vintage of your vehicle, and the presence (or lack thereof) of jingle in your pocket. A perfectly acceptable fender, door, or other necessary parts can often be as close as your local salvage yard, for prices that are considerably less than new replacement parts. To go this route, you are well advised to know what years your particular make and model will accept before you start searching the salvage yards. If you need a left front fender for a 1996 Whizbang Whatzit, you will be more apt to find what you need if you know that the front fenders are the same for that model as the ones manufactured between years 1991 and 1999. Of course, knowing that the hood hinge mechanism was mounted to the fender differently starting in 1995 will save you some grief as well.

Salvage Parts

If you resort to buying a replacement panel from a salvage yard, try to find the best sheet metal available that will fit your vehicle. Buying a replacement panel that needs more work (such as collision repair or rust repair) than what you already have is simply defeating your purpose. Chances are, you won't be able to find a door or fender that fits or is the same color as your car, but you can take care of those points easily enough. If you are doing paintwork on adjacent panels, painting a door or fender won't take much more work.

Consider having the salvage yard panel you pick up chemically dipped or media-blasted, if necessary, *before* you begin installation on your vehicle. Whether you're buying new or used parts, verify that any necessary mounting brackets, emblems, or trim are included with your purchase, and that they are still in usable condition for your vehicle.

Reconditioned Parts

Mechanical parts that were damaged in an accident can generally be replaced by reconditioned parts. You can also purchase these items—for example,

starters, alternators, radiators, fuel tanks, and similar items—new or from a salvage yard, with the price you pay reflecting their source.

DETERMINING THE REQUIRED LABOR

If you are going to be able to do all of the work required for this repair, your labor cost is simply the price of your time. Of course, everyone knows that you can't charge yourself for your own time, so in a sense you aren't going to make any money on the deal. However, before you decide to dive in and perform the repair, you should figure out what your time is going to cost you.

Do It Yourself

To do the work yourself, you need to devote a certain amount of time to the project or it simply won't be completed. If this is a second car that doesn't have to be repaired immediately (as your daily driver would), you can be a little more flexible with your time. Is it feasible to devote the greatest part of the next few weekends or your after-work time to getting the car repaired? If the answer is no, you may need to have the work done professionally. If you do have the time, though, you will surely save some money.

Subcontract

Even if you have the time to do the repair, and you possess the skills to do the bodywork required, you may still need to subcontract some of the work. Some of this work may be minor, while some may be substantial. Before you perform any actual repairs on the vehicle yourself, check the body shops in your local area to be sure that the outsourced services you will need are available and approximately how much they will cost you.

Chassis or Unibody Straightening

If the chassis or unibody shell is bent, the only way to make it correct again is to have is straightened on a frame straightening table. Most professional auto body repair shops have the equipment to do this, or they can recommend a shop that does.

The basic process for frame straightening is to drive or winch the vehicle on the rack, take measurements at specific locations with precise measuring equipment, and then pull the chassis or unibody back into correct alignment by using hydraulic jacks that are part of the frame straightening table. This frame straightening process squares up the chassis. Don't confuse this process with wheel alignment, which aligns the wheels to the chassis.

Mechanical Repair

When body panels are damaged in an automobile accident, it is quite possible that mechanical items will also be damaged and require repair or replacement. An auto body repair shop can typically complete some of these services, while other repairs may call for work by a mechanic. Auto body repair shops can install a new radiator, recharge an air conditioning system, or perform various other tasks that simply require bolting on a new part.

Since the vehicle being repaired is yours, there is no rule against making all the repairs yourself. Your decision will depend on your automotive knowledge and experience, availability of tools and equipment, and your willingness and ability to learn new tasks. However, if you don't have everything you need to repair the vehicle so that it is safe and reliable, send that portion you can't handle to a professional.

Glass Replacement

Besides sheet metal and radiators, the other most vulnerable component in an automobile accident is the window glass. Replace any glass that is cracked or broken, especially if it impedes the driver's field of vision through the front windshield. Replacement glass can be obtained through your local automotive glass shop.

Installing glass is not as difficult as you might think, but, since the material is fragile, making a mistake could cost you more money than you will save by doing it yourself. Incorrect installation can get the glass in a bind, which makes it susceptible to cracking or breaking, while improper sealing can cause leaks. Depending on your skills and comfort level, glass installation is one part of the repair that you may want to subcontract. For more on glass replacement, see Chapter 6.

Chapter 4
Disassembly & Stripping

Most auto body repair requires a certain amount of disassembly, whether fixing damage due to a collision or merely serving to restore an older vehicle. A methodical approach to this process is essential, no matter if the parts are being replaced or repaired and refinished, or you are simply taking apart the affected area to gain better access to other parts.

Additionally, some sheet metal parts may require stripping off old finishes in order to obtain the best possible results with the new applications of body filler and/or paint. You can perform this removal of paint or rust with media blasting, chemical dipping, or by grinding and sanding.

DISASSEMBLY
Take your time and think about what you are doing. This will save you a self-inflicted headache if you go about simply unbolting everything haphazardly and pay

As seen in this photo, both front fenders, the grille, bumper, headlights, and all related front-end components have been removed. Whether they are being replaced or repaired, you can bet that each piece will be retained until the entire vehicle is refinished and reassembled to verify that all nuts, bolts, and emblems are reinstalled as if the vehicle had never been damaged.

3

After removing all of the bolts from the deflector, the bumper/fascia assembly is typically still secured by fasteners into the front fenders. With these bolts removed, the bumper/fascia assembly can be slid forward and removed. Since the material is much lighter than sheet metal assemblies, it usually requires just one person to remove it.

(continued)

4

After the bumper/fascia assembly is removed, additional damaged pieces can be removed. Using a pneumatic ratchet will speed the process, but this tool is not a required for this kind of repair. Disassembly is simply a matter of looking for and removing all of the fasteners that appear to be holding the particular piece in place. If it still does not come off, keep looking for the remaining fastener, just as professional body men are required to do.

5

In this particular case, the hood release cable has to be disconnected from the latch prior to removing the latch assembly.

6

A body man will spot poor design at once: this hood release cable passes through a hole in the panel at the top of the photo. To remove this panel, the release cable will need to be removed. Additionally, it most likely will need to pass back through this same hole upon reassembly to reach its destination and operate correctly.

continued from page 49

resealable plastic food storage bags. Include all of the bulbs, mounting bolts, or whatever other loose items may be related to this item in the bag as well. In instances where there are multiple parts that look alike, you will do well to place a tag directly on the bag or inside of it, with information that give the specifics of this particular component. Other labels, such as "left taillight/right taillight" or "one of four," "two of four," and so on, will help to make correct reassembly easier. Of course, any of these labels or notes may be referenced in the disassembly notes you make as you rip them off the vehicle.

Some components will not fit in food storage bags, but you can use the same methodology to store these parts in small storage boxes. You can find new storage boxes in a variety of sizes at your local office supply store. Boxes are easier to stack, making them a potentially better alternative to plastic storage bags.

Large Parts

Larger components, such as fenders, hoods, doors, obviously will not fit into bags or boxes. These items should be set on the floor or shelf in a manner that prevents them from falling and causing damage to themselves or other components. Situate these parts so that they are easy to reach and move when you are ready for them. If a part requires two people to move it, place it where two people can get to it; this will avoid damage to the part and prevent personal injury to yourself or others.

If possible, reinstall all mounting hardware in the component where it belongs, or place the mounting hardware in a bag or box and label it accordingly. Again, reference this storage info with your disassembly notes to avoid last-minute trips to the hardware store for scrounging up mounting bolts during the reassembly process.

Labeling

You may think you'll remember where each and every nut or bolt goes on this vehicle. However, you will most likely forget some of them before you're ready for reinstallation. This is much more likely in the case of a hot rod buildup or muscle car restoration. If you label everything in the beginning, though, you will be glad you did.

STRIPPING

There's a stripper in southern Indiana I have visited a few times who has received a fair amount of money from me. There are some things that a man needs done that simply call for a stripper. Now, before you think I have slipped to the immoral side, let me tell you that it was all on the up and up. Of course, in my case I'm talking about having paint and rust removed from a Model A Tudor and an old Chevy truck.

Stripping is commonly used when a vehicle is being completely rebuilt, rather than when repair is necessitated by a collision. However, it is certainly worth mentioning this any time you consider bodywork. If the underlying paint is incompatible with the new top coats of paint to be applied, if there is significant rust—or any time you just don't know about the integrity of the sheet metal and its multiple layers of who-knows-what—the panel should be stripped to bare metal for the best results.

When it was commonly used, lacquer paint could be applied in as many coats as you wanted to achieve some of the deepest, shiniest paint jobs ever seen. While this was acceptable for vehicles that were used only on the show car circuit, whenever those multiple coats of lacquer were exposed to the elements for any amount of time, they would begin to look like sunburned alligator skin. To repaint a vehicle in this condition, all of the paint must be removed, down to bare metal. Lacquer paint is hardly ever used now, but there are countless vehicles housed in barns and garages that have been painted with lacquer and are more than suitable for restoration.

It can be difficult to distinguish accurately between surface rust and rust-through when looking at a possible hot rod or restoration project. The only real way to tell what's good and what isn't is to strip down to bare metal. Then you can see if you can install a patch panel to resurrect the piece in question or if you need to replace the entire piece. Of course, depending on how obvious the rust is and the availability of a patch panel, you may be better off saving your money and purchasing a new panel.

Stripping is appropriate in auto body repair anytime you have a used sheet metal component that will replace a damaged component. This is not as much of a problem on newer vehicles, but it may be possible that the donor vehicle has been in fender-benders prior to its present condition as a total wreck, relegated to the salvage yard. There could be various layers of paint intermingled with various layers of good or bad body filler beneath what looks like a decent coat of paint. The last thing you want is to complete all of the other repair/repaint work on your vehicle, just to have a replaced fender or other panel begin to deteriorate soon after finishing the job. Again, any time you have doubts or concerns about what is beneath the paint, the only way you know for sure is to strip it all off.

After sanding the first layer of paint off this early Camaro's front fender, it is quite obvious that the car had been a different color at one time. Additionally, there is evidence of some body filler that may not have been applied correctly. This is a good example of why stripping to bare metal is a good idea if you do not know the full history of the vehicle.

This sports car body has been stripped of all paint, most likely by some sort of media blasting. The interior has been masked off and the body is ready for an application of self-etching or epoxy primer to protect it from the reoccurrence of rust. For the body to be chemically dipped, the body would need to be removed from the chassis/suspension, then primed prior to being reinstalled on the chassis.

There are three basic methods for stripping paint and rust from automobiles. In no particular order, they are media blasting, chemical stripping, and grinding or sanding. Each has benefits and drawbacks, related expenses—and horror stories.

Media Blasting

For a long time, coarse river sand was widely used for media blasting, which is why it is often known as sandblasting, an outdated term. Sand can be used for removing graffiti from steel bridges, masonry structures, and various other surfaces. However, sand can quickly put heavy scratches into something lighter and will produce significant heat on application, causing sheet metal panels to warp. Silica sand is much finer than river sand, though it has drawbacks as well. Using any kind of sand for blasting purposes will create an extremely fine dust, which is known to cause silicosis. Avoid this extremely nasty side effect by using one of a number of alternative products.

In lieu of sandblasting, media blasting offers a great way to remove paint, peeling chrome, and rust. However, you can't simply start blasting away at your parts. Three very important steps to start with when prepping for media blasting are (1) mask the area that should not be blasted, (2) use the appropriate blasting media, and (3) remove all of the blasting media when the job is complete. You must also wear proper safety apparel, including eye and respiratory protection.

Masking

No matter what type of media is used, media blasting will leave a slightly textured surface. For this reason, machined surfaces, bearing surfaces, threaded areas, or any other areas that might be affected negatively by this should be masked from media blasting. Exterior threads, such as those on the back of some trim pieces, can be protected from blasting easily by covering them with a length of appropriately sized rubber hose or tubing. Other areas can be masked with heavy cardboard and masking tape, accompanied by the prudent use of lower blasting pressure and a careful aim.

Media Selection

The blasting media should be compatible with the material on which it is being used. If it is harder than the prepped surface, you will do more harm than good by hurling hard objects at it. A large volume of softer material passing by the surface is a more appropriate

way of freeing the surface of unwanted material such as paint or rust. These softer materials typically include silica sand, aluminum oxide, plastic media, or walnut shells. Avoid using steel shot media or coarse river sand.

Various materials other than sand can be used for media blasting. No one material is the best for all stripping or cleanup operations, so be sure to match the media with the task. Aluminum oxide is a good choice for removing paint and rust from steel. Plastic media is a little more expensive, though it is the best for stripping paint from metal, as it doesn't get as hot and cause warping. Glass bead blasting does a good job on most any surface, though it's not the all-around best media for cleanup projects. For cleaning soft metals such as aluminum, die cast, or brass, aluminum shot is best, although it is more expensive.

When choosing a blasting media, remember that any scratches or abrasions that you put into the metal while cleaning it will also need to be removed. An aggressive media will no doubt remove paint and other finishes faster, but if the media is harder than the material being blasted, you will get to a point where you are creating more work for yourself.

This chart on page 57 gives media and air pressure settings recommendations for various blasting projects.

Media Removal

In addition to the flaking rust, paint, or whatever else was on the part prior to blasting, you must also remove all of the blasting media once you have finished blasting. Much of the media used for blasting is recycled and used again. Remember that, even if your parts were not oily or greasy, previously blasted parts may have been. Any oil that is present on your parts will cause adhesion problems, so it is imperative that you clean all parts thoroughly after they have been media-blasted.

A drawback to media blasting is that the media can be difficult to remove from confined areas. It is fine for use on a simple two-sided surface such as a fender. However, on a door shell, pickup truck cab, or passenger car body, some of the media will collect between panels and will be difficult to remove. If the media stays in hiding, it may not present a significant problem, but it may decide to come out when you are in the middle of spraying the perfect top coat of paint. Years ago, I had the cab of a 1951 Chevrolet pickup sandblasted. In those particular trucks, the roof area is a double-wall construction, but the back panel is single-wall. As you might predict, a lot of very fine sand found its way

BLAST MEDIA	SURFACE MATERIAL	TYPE OF BLASTING	RECOMMENDED AIR PRESSURE (PSI)
Glass Bead	Aluminum, brass, die cast	Cleaning	60
Aluminum Oxide	Steel	Removal of rust and paint; increases adhesion of paint or powder coating	80–90
Silicon Carbide	Steel	Preparation for welding	80–90
Walnut Shells	Engine/transmission assemblies	Cleaning	80
Plastic Media	Sheet metal	Paint removal	30–90
Plastic Media	Aluminum, brass, die cast	Cleaning	80–90

This table serves as a guide to what media should be used on various materials and the recommended air pressure to use for each.

between the roof panels. Since I never got around to finishing the interior, nothing kept all of that sand in the roof: I got a light sprinkling of sand every time I hit a bump in the road.

Chemical Stripping

The chemical removal of paint and rust can be done at home or you can have it done commercially. The amount of stripping and the availability of a chemical stripper in your area will most likely be the key points to consider when considering this type of work. If you have several parts or a number of large pieces to be stripped, it will be more practical to strip them commercially. If you simply need to strip one or two pieces or just one salvage yard fender, for instance, you can do this yourself.

Chemical stripping doesn't work well on thick plastic body filler, so if you have a panel that you know contains body filler, remove as much of it as you can before attempting to strip it chemically. This can be accomplished simply using a 36-grit disc on an orbital sander. If thick body filler is not removed before the panel is chemically stripped, the filler will begin to peel but not come off completely. The body filler will prevent the stripper from actually stripping the surface beneath the filler, making the entire process a waste of time.

Regardless of brand, paint stripper in general is some pretty nasty stuff. Be sure to follow all safety precautions on the product label. As someone who has stripped a complete pickup truck by hand with paint stripper, I strongly recommend that you wear rubber gloves, a respirator, thick shoes or boots, long pants, and long-sleeve shirt. If you accidently drop some paint stripper on bare skin, you will quickly wish that you hadn't. While the burning goes away after a while, it will serve as a reminder that, at the absolute minimum, you should cover as much of your skin as possible and wear long rubber gloves.

The one thing that the instructions for paint stripper don't tell you is that you should scuff the painted surface with 36- or 50-grit sandpaper prior to applying the stripper. Decently applied paint will fight the stripper if the surface is not scuffed to ease penetration of the stripper. Scuffing the surface first allows you to use less stripper and save time in the actual stripping process.

When using paint stripper, place the vehicle or parts on a concrete surface that can be hosed down with water after the stripping process. After scuffing the painted surface, spread the paint stripper on with a paintbrush, then wait while the stripper works its way through the multiple layers of paint and primer. As the paint begins to bubble up, peel the softened paint from the surface with a metal scraper or razor blade; additional paint stripper can be applied to stubborn spots.

When all of the paint has been removed from the panel, the stripper must be neutralized before proceeding with bodywork or applications of body filler or primer. Unless the particular stripper you use calls for a different method of neutralization, lots of water should take care of this. However, you must contain the runoff and dispose of it properly and according to

continued on page 61

HOW TO MEDIA-BLAST A TRUCK CAB

My most recent automotive project was a 1955 Chevrolet pickup that I purchased sight unseen (save for a few snapshots) via the Internet. Since my first car was a similar 1957 GMC pickup, this project is near and dear to my heart, as I plan to keep the truck forever. Therefore, I wanted to take my time and get it built to the absolute best of my abilities. Even though the truck was from California, it had various patches of rust in some places. The cab had suffered some damage to the driver's side rear corner, which was not repaired very well due to a significant angle point in what should be a flat back panel. Considering this situation, I believed the cab should be stripped of all paint in order to thoroughly address the health of the cab's sheet metal.

Before having the cab sandblasted, I already knew that the rocker panels and steps and the door hinge pockets were a bit soft. I had my 1957 GMC pickup in high school; since then, the aftermarket has flourished and many more parts are available for these trucks now than they were back then. For this project, sheet metal parts were readily available, so I could replace the A-pillars, rocker panels, doors, and back panel.

After dismantling the cab as completely as possible, I took it to Chris Riedel Sandblasting. Using very fine sand, all paint, primer, and rust was removed from the cab. There were some areas where some crude repairs were made in the past, using very thick applications of plastic body filler. Due to the thickness, this could not be removed completely. However, my next step as part of the new repair work was to remove the body filler.

1

A fresh coat of paint or even primer can often hide a multitude of bodywork sins for a while, but even in primer, it was evident that this truck cab required significant work. Doors, front fenders, rocker panels and steps, along with the rear cab panel, all must be replaced.

The windshield glass, gauges, gas tank, and anything else that could come out of the cab was removed before stripping.

2

3

Unlike some vehicles, there were not too many surprises when the cab came back from being sandblasted. The panels (rocker panels in particular) to be repaired looked a bit worse, but nothing catastrophic showed up. Had the cab been chemically stripped, the surface would have been smooth and relatively shiny, just as new bare metal. The sandblasted surface appears with a slight texture.

(continued)

HOW TO MEDIA-BLAST A TRUCK CAB *(CONTINUED)*

One issue around the forward cab mounts raised some concern once the primer and rust were removed. These mounts are certainly not as solid as hoped for, as evidenced by the daylight around this one on the passenger side. Now the choice is to replace the entire toeboard or weld in some smaller localized patches.

Regardless of the method used to strip any sheet metal body or component, it should be protected by a couple of coats of epoxy primer as soon as feasible to prevent the re-formation of rust due to humidity. There is still a lot of work ahead on this cab, but with the strong aftermarket, it can be repaired to better than new condition. However, new cabs are available for this make and model as well.

With no paint or primer on this hot rod, it's easy to determine what bodywork still needs to be done. While much of it already has been done and the body looks to be in pretty decent shape, closer inspection will quickly show that the job is not yet completed. Many climates are not conducive to keeping a vehicle body in bare metal for very long, but, if possible, an uncovered body will reveal any damage that should be repaired.

continued from page 49

local codes. Check with your source of paint stripper for recommendations on disposing the used stripper that you rinse from the parts you have just stripped.

Although I would never again try stripping a complete car or truck by hand, any one part of a vehicle is considerably smaller and therefore requires a less involved stripping effort. If you need to remove paint from one fender or a smaller panel, a gallon of paint stripper should be enough.

Commercial Dipping

If you have numerous parts or large pieces (including complete body shells) to be stripped, having them dipped commercially is the most practical approach. For the best results, the pieces and parts should be disassembled as completely as possible and any large amounts of body filler removed. Large parts will be dipped individually, while small parts will be placed into a basket and then dipped.

The parts being stripped first go into a "hot tank" that is filled with a caustic solution. This removes

A closer look at the same car shows that there are still some small rust-through spots and some rust pitting. While the rust-through should be welded shut or a small panel cut in, some high build primer and a fair amount of block sanding will cover the pitting.

wax, grease, and paint from the metal. This step lasts from four to eight hours, depending on the amount of buildup on the metal. When the wax, grease, and paint is gone, the metal is pulled from the "hot tank"

TOP: A fender or hood (or smaller pieces) can be stripped chemically with relative ease if you just have a few parts or do not have access to a commercial stripper. The materials to do so are usually as close as your local auto parts store. Although not completely finished in the photo, this truck hood was completely stripped on a Saturday morning.

BOTTOM: Dual-action (DA) sanders have been a staple of the bodywork business for a long time. Depending on the grit of the sanding disc that is applied, it will quickly remove paint and primer from an area to be repaired or excess body filler from an area that is being filled.

and rinsed with plain water for three to four hours to remove all of the caustic solution.

The next step places the metal parts into a second vat filled with de-rusting solution. While in this solution to remove rust, the material is connected to an electrical charge. Unlike chrome plating and powder coating, both of which use an electric charge to draw chrome or powder material to the metal, the de-rusting process reverses the current. Iron oxide molecules (that is, rust) are drawn away from the metal and separate themselves from the good metal. Depending on the condition of the metal and the amount of rust, this step can take 20 to 40 hours. When the remaining metal is removed from the de-rusting vat, the parts are thoroughly rinsed again with plain water to neutralize any remaining de-rusting solution.

Parts that are chemically stripped should be primed with epoxy primer as soon as practical to prevent the formation of surface rust. A benefit or drawback of chemical dipping is that the stripping solution touches all surfaces of the parts that are immersed. This will remove all rust, but may leave areas of good metal with no protection if you can't reach them later to apply epoxy primer and paint or undercoating.

Grinding/Sanding

If you simply need to get down to bare metal on a few parts in a localized area, an electric or pneumatic orbital sander will do the job sufficiently. By using a 36-grit sanding disc, you can remove old body filler or previous layers of paint and primer very quickly,

exactly in the places you want to reach. This can often be done in less time than what it would take to load the parts in a truck and bring them to a media blaster or chemical stripping facility.

However, you should limit this method to relatively small, localized areas, as the process creates a lot of heat that can warp otherwise perfectly good panels. Don't try removing paint from an entire vehicle with a sander: the heat this will invariably produce will cause significant warping, you'll go through several sanding discs, and this process will simply take too much time. Even when used to strip a small area, the sanding disc should be moved around instead of holding the sander in one spot. You should also hold the sander so that the sanding disc flexes slightly, rather than flat against the surfaces being stripped.

Chapter 5
Collision Repair: Metal

Repairing bent sheet metal components is a relatively simple, five-step process. Remove the paint from the area to be repaired, straighten the deformed sheet metal as much as possible, apply a skim coat of filler to perfect the surface shape, prime, and then paint.

PANEL REPAIR

In theory, dent repair is very simple. However, inexperienced body men often make the job more difficult than it needs to be. The thinking goes that, since the initial impact was significant to make a dent as big and deep as it is, it must take the same amount of force to straighten it out. The body man then picks up the biggest, heaviest hammer from his tool chest and proceeds to whale the tar out of the damaged sheet metal from the opposite side. Now, admittedly, it may require a big hammer and a couple of hefty swings, but if you don't know what you're doing, you are more likely to create more damage than fix the dent.

The correct way to remove a dent is to essentially "undo" the damage. That is, hammer the dent out in the opposite progression of the way that it happened. On a simple dent, produced for example by a baseball hitting the middle of a panel, this is a simple task to undo. In a collision, however, assessing the dent is usually more involved.

When two vehicles collide, or your car strikes a tree or utility pole, dents become much more complex. During the initial impact, the sheet metal is pushed inward. Since it is a formed piece that has been stamped into a predetermined shape, like a fender, there are already some built-in forces present in the metal. When these forces are combined with the force of the impact, the sheet metal surrounding the initial point of contact typically bulges outward in reaction.

In this simple example, the repair process calls for hammering the bulging sheet metal back into place. Then, hammer the dented sheet metal back out from the inside or pull it back out from the outside.

Automotive collisions are not that simple, though, since the actual crash is rarely limited to a single point of impact. One vehicle's bumper will hit the other vehicle in a fender, while the fender of the first vehicle hits the door of the second vehicle or some other similar scenario. The point is that the entire damage should be repaired sequentially, in the reverse order of how the initial damage happened. This doesn't mean that you must repair the door before you repair the fender, but the dents in each individual panel should be addressed in the opposite order of how they occurred. To proceed differently will cause you more work, as you will actually be stretching the metal and causing more damage to the sheet metal.

Dolly-On/Dolly-Off Hammering

In most situations, using a hammer by itself (without a dolly behind the metal) will merely cause a larger than desired area of metal to move inward, which is not the desired effect when repairing a dent in sheet metal. By using a dolly behind the panel and a

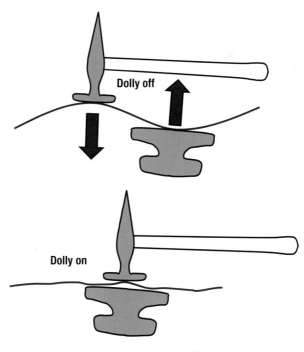

This exaggerated drawing should explain the differences between dolly-off and dolly-on hammering. The basic distinction concerns the relationship between the position of the body hammer and the body dolly, when striking a piece of sheet metal.

hammer in front of the panel, the sheet metal can be worked in a more predictable manner, as the dolly focuses the force of the hammer.

Dollies are used in two basic ways: dolly on or dolly off. When hammering on the dolly, the dolly is located behind the sheet metal and directly beneath the hammer blow. This method knocks down high spots or smoothes ripples within the relatively small size of the dolly. Hammering off the dolly is done by hitting the surface of the panel adjacent to the dolly, rather than directly on it. This causes the dolly to push outward while the hammer pushes inward, a method typically used on larger areas of repair.

Door Repair

Anytime a door is damaged in a collision, the person making the repair may have to deal with more than just damaged sheet metal. The very nature of the door, as a movable component, may lead you to replace, repair, or,

at a minimum, adjust the door's hinges and/or the latch mechanisms. Additionally, you may have broken door glass to remove and replace, as well as window riser mechanisms. On a bare-bones automobile, that may be the extent of the repair work. But on higher level vehicles, damage can occur to door-mounted remote controls, stereo speakers, and now, more commonly, side-curtain airbags. If the exterior of the door is damaged sufficiently, the interior door panel may be damaged as well. None of these additional tasks are beyond home repair: they simply add opportunities to gain first-hand body repair experience.

Doors and Door Skins

Since automobile doors consist of two basic components—a mostly hollow inner panel and an outer skin—some door repairs can be made by simply re-skinning the door. Before you attempt these repairs, consider the following.

continued on page 77

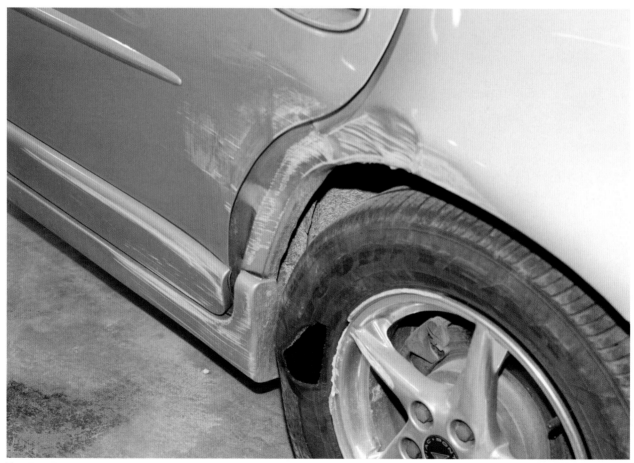

For orientation, this is the left rear wheel on a four door sedan. The rear quarter panel and door each need a slide hammer to pull them, followed by the addition of some body filler. Both the wheel and tire need to be replaced.

This damage is too deep to cover with filler alone, but access to the backside with a body hammer is very limited. Using a stud gun (described elsewhere) would allow these panels to be pulled back to fairly close to original shape. A skim coat of plastic body filler could then be added to finish the repair prior to primer and paint.

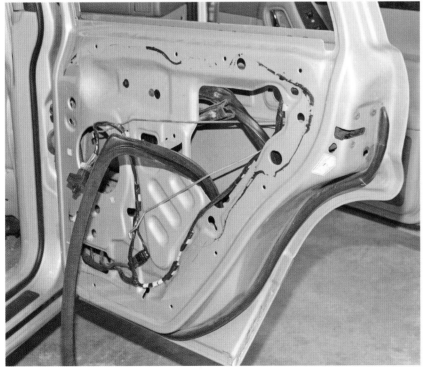

This door has already been repaired, but the glass needs to be reinstalled, the window riser mechanism connected, and the interior panel installed. The thick black rubber is actually a portion of the molding that fits around the glass, but has simply been stuck inside the door for safekeeping until the glass is reinstalled. Keeping track of parts during repair is important.

HOW TO REPAIR A GROUP OF DENTS

In the world of auto body repair, we see everything from minor dents and dings to high-impact collisions. Home repairs can fix most of this kind of damage. Simple dents commonly occur in a parking lot, on wet or icy roads, or sometimes in your own driveway.

Although there may be points of impact on multiple panels, no panels require replacement or realignment. They merely need to be straightened out and refinished. To get the low-down on these common repairs, follow along as one of the body men from Jerry's Auto Body straightens some metal and performs some body filling prior to prepping for paint. The dents in the doors are shallow enough to be filled, while the rear quarter needs to be straightened and then perfected with a skim coat of filler.

This Dodge sedan suffered some minor damage to the driver side doors and rear quarter panel. None of the damage was severe, and most of it could be repaired by a hobbyist. Careful attention to detail during the body repair and prep work will go a long way toward making this sedan look like new, once the repairs are completed.

This photo shows the original damage before any metal straightening has been done. Where metal work is required and filler will be applied, the paint is removed completely by using a DA sander. Outside of this area, paint is removed, but the original primer or sealer is left intact. These two areas will receive the heaviest coatings of primer-surfacer, although it will be built up in thin layers, rather than in one thick coat. The large gray area has been scuffed lightly to offer good adhesion, though the original sealer is still intact.

3

This sedan's damage is typical of the sort of easy repairs a hobbyist can perform without relative ease. It consisted of a few small dents in the doors and rear quarter panel. No metal was creased or torn, and no glass was broken. Even if your sheet metal straightening skills are not the best, most of these repairs could be filled with body filler to a satisfactory degree. A deeper dent would simply take more layers of filler, as each application of filler cannot be very thick.

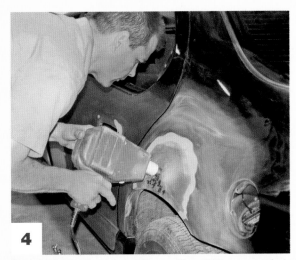

4

To straighten sheet metal, you often need to pull it to remove a dent. To make this easier, this stud welder is used to temporarily weld small metal rods (about ⅛ inch diameter and 2½ inches long) to the sheet metal.

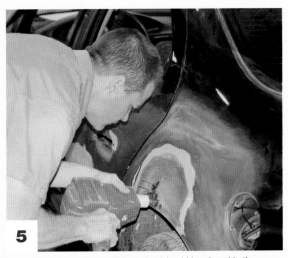

5

To make the studs most efficient, they should be placed in the deepest areas of the damage. Additional studs should then be placed in areas that are not as deep.

(continued)

HOW TO REPAIR A GROUP OF DENTS *(CONTINUED)*

6 A slide hammer can be slid over the rods one at a time, then slid out to pull the sheet metal into its correct position. Sometimes a hammer may need to be used to tap the metal back in slightly if it was pulled out too far.

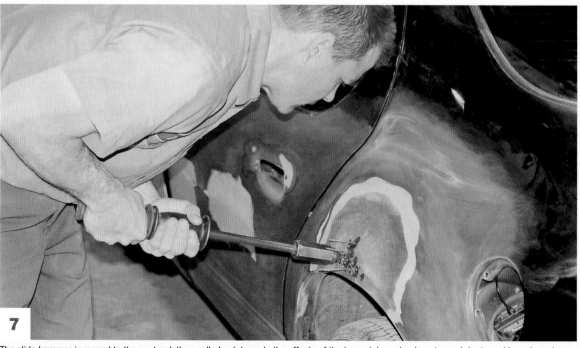

7 The slide hammer is moved to the next rod, then pulled out, to undo the effects of the impact. Learning how to read dents and knowing where to pull is an art that takes practice. Typically, the deepest portion of the dent is pulled out first, followed by the lesser dents. As long as none of the studs are removed, you can go back and pull previously pulled studs more, if necessary.

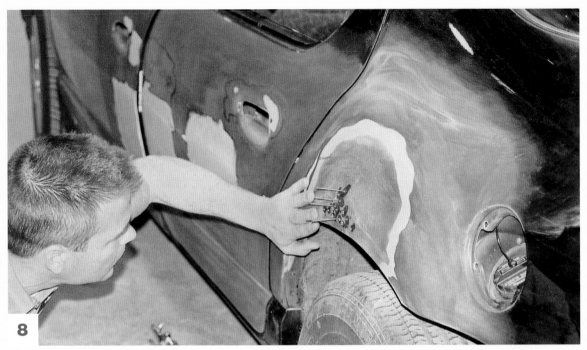

8 After some pulling, progress is checked to verify that the panel has been returned to its proper contour. Return the panel as closely as possible to its original shape, though you don't want any of the panel to be too high. High spots will need to be hammered back down (prior to application of filler), while subtle low spots can be filled.

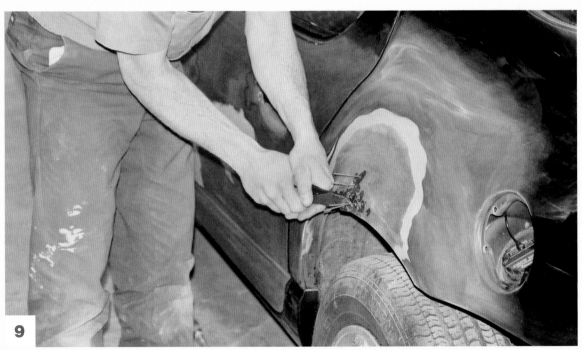

9 With the pulling completed, the rods can be cut off as close to the body as possible with a pair of diagonal cutters.

(continued)

COLLISION REPAIR: METAL

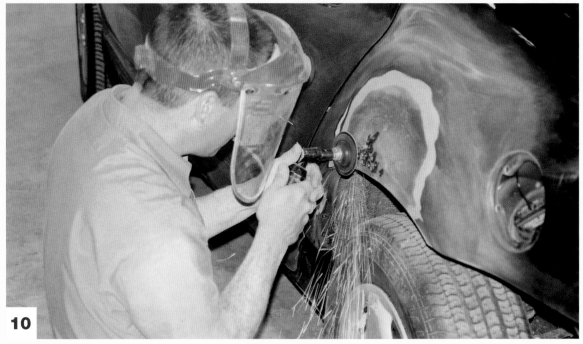

10

The stubs are then ground away with a grinder and a coarse disc.

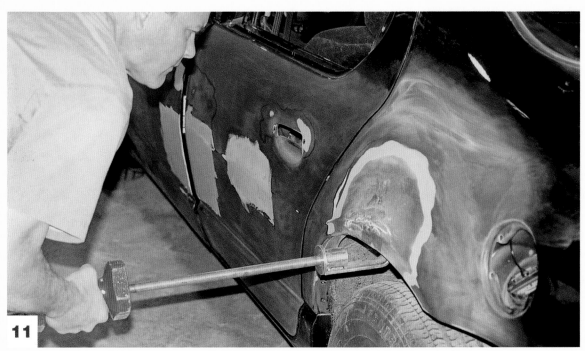

11

The lip of the fender has been determined to be slightly low, so it is pulled out using the slide hammer and a fender lip attachment.

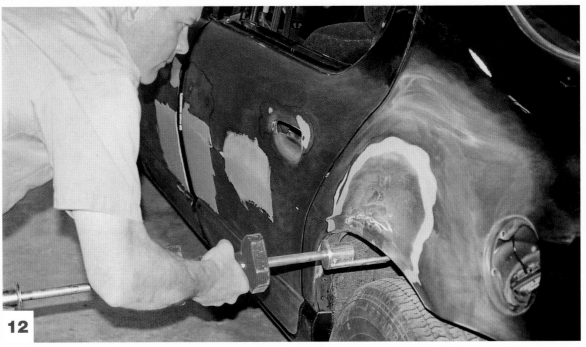

12

A couple of more tugs with the slide hammer and it should be pretty close.

13

A slight high spot is finessed back into place, using a small hammer. Older vehicles generally have thicker sheet metal, while newer vehicles generally have thinner, more pliable sheet metal. The amount of brute strength and finesse necessary depend on the vintage of the vehicle.

(continued)

HOW TO REPAIR A GROUP OF DENTS *(CONTINUED)*

14

Prior to the application of any body filler, the various layers of sheet metal, primer, and paint are quite evident on the rear quarter panel of this sedan. The very smallest dark area is where small rods were temporarily welded to the panel for use with the slide hammer to straighten the dent. The next larger area is where the paint has been sanded off to expose bare metal. Outside of this, the original primer or sealer can be used beneath the factory paint. Next is the paint, which has been scuffed to enhance adhesion of the primer-surfacer, and, finally, the untouched original painted surface.

15

A mixing board with disposable tear-off sheets is great for mixing body filler. Appropriate amounts of filler and hardener are mixed together using a plastic spreader. After the filler is spread, the sheet is torn off and disposed of, providing a clean surface for mixing the next batch of filler.

16

Using a flexible spreader and a careful eye, the filler is spread to fill any low spots. Care must be taken to minimize air bubbles. When the filler hardens, it can then be sanded to its final shape with 80- or 100-grit sandpaper.

17

After using a slide hammer to straighten the metal to very near its original contour, two or three thin coats of body filler are applied to match the final contour. If pinholes are present after sanding the body filler, glazing putty can be used to fill them.

(continued)

18 These areas of body filler show that the actual damaged areas to this sedan were really four small dents (two in each driver side door) and a larger dent above the left rear wheel. If they were repainted separately, this car would look like a spotted leopard, so the entire side will be repainted.

19 The doors on this sedan are relatively straight in the front-to-back direction, while they are contoured from top to bottom. To maintain this straightness, a long sanding board is used to sand front-to-back, while moving up and down along the door.

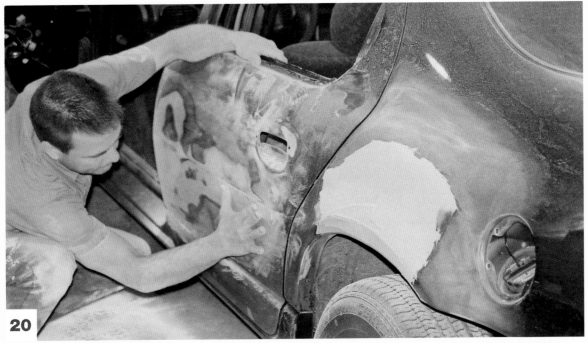

20

Due to the irregular pressure of your hand, do not sand without using some type of sanding block. Using your hand alone with tend to make the panel wavy, as more pressure will be applied by your fingers and less in the area in between them. However, checking your progress while sanding by taking the time to feel the sanded panel with your hand will give a good indication of high and low spots.

21

Be sure to use an air hose occasionally to remove any buildup of body filler dust.

(continued)

HOW TO REPAIR A GROUP OF DENTS *(CONTINUED)*

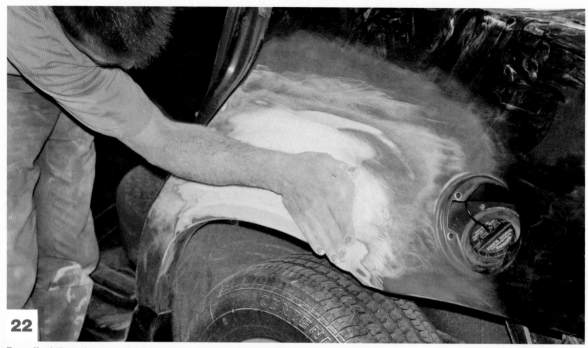

22 To scuff existing paint or as a final smoothing effort, you can use Scotch-Brite pads. Available in three different levels of coarseness, the coarsest is appropriate for scuffing paint before applying a sealer, while the finest works for final smoothing prior to applying primer-surfacer.

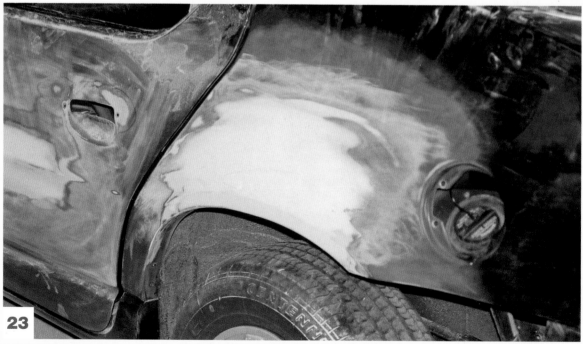

23 Looking at this filled area after sanding has been completed, we can tell that filler (pale yellow) was used to cover the larger area, and a slight amount of glaze (light blue) was used to finish the edge of the wheelwell.

continued from page 64

First and foremost, this repair will be beneficial only if the original inner panel is still undamaged (or at least straight). If the collision impact caused damage to the inner panel, which cannot be easily repaired, you should consider finding a replacement door. Likewise, if the outer skin is damaged due to rust, you should verify that the inner panel is still structurally sound. It may be usable, but it might actually be in worse shape than the outer skin.

If the inner panel is still usable, you should determine if an outer skin is available for your vehicle's make and model. If it is, you are in luck, as a door skin will be considerably less expensive than a replacement door. Of course, if this is your daily driver, you may choose to replace the entire door while you're at it.

If you decide to replace the door skin, the following steps should be taken. First, remove the door from the vehicle, the internal components from the inside of the door, and then set the door atop a pair of sawhorses or other suitable work stand.

The original door skin is secured by the edges wrapping around the flange of the inner door panel. To remove it, use a grinder along the edge of the door to separate the main part of the door skin from the part that flaps over. When this is completed, you should be able to remove the skin. If it can't be removed, there may be spot welds around the flange that must be drilled out. Once you have done this, you should now be able to remove the outer skin. You will also need to remove the part that flaps over from the inside of the inner door panel.

To install a new skin, first double-check to make sure that no fragments of the previous door skin, any spot welds, or panel adhesive remain on the surface to which the new skin will be applied. Then position the new skin so that the excess "skin" is centered front to back and top to bottom. Using a permanent marker or a scribe, make some positioning reference marks on the inside of the door skin so that it can be placed in this position again. Then remove the door skin, apply a bead of panel adhesive to the inside of the door skin and to the mating surface on the inner door panel. Allow the panel adhesive to get slightly tacky, then press the door skin into position. Use clamps to secure the door skin in place. You can use C-clamps, clamping pliers (Vise-Grips), or other types of clamps. However, be sure to take the appropriate precautions to avoid damaging the new door skin or inner panel. After the two panels are clamped together, wipe away any excess panel adhesive that oozes from inside the door.

After the panel adhesive has set (refer to the product label for the time this will take), the edges of the door skin still need to be folded over the edge of the inner door panel. There are several ways to do this and even more tools available to do it. Some body men use door-skinning pliers to fold the edge over, while others use duckbill locking pliers. After the edge is folded over somewhat, it must be pressed down flat against the inside of the door panel. Some use a light door-skinning hammer, while others use a mallet or a smooth-faced body hammer and a dolly. This is one of those cases where there are several ways to perform the same task, depending on what tools you have available and how you use them. The main thing to remember is that the edge of the door skin must be flat against the inner panel, but you don't want to do any damage to the outer side.

Hinges

Although some vehicles may have three hinges on each door, two hinges per door are more common. Regardless of the number of hinges, the pivot point for all hinges on any door must be aligned for the door to operate properly. If any of the hinges have become misaligned during an accident (or possibly due to rust, if the vehicle has been sitting for a long time), the door simply will not open and close as it should.

If you determine that one of the hinges is misaligned, you need to determine which half of it needs repair or adjustment. Half of the hinge attaches to the door, while the other half attaches to the door pillar. If the door pillar appears to be intact but the door itself has suffered an impact, the door half of the hinge will be suspect. Conversely, if the door is unscathed but the door pillar has sustained damage, you will most likely need to repair or adjust the hinge at the door pillar. On most, but certainly not all, vehicles, the door pillar portion of the hinge has less adjustability. Any adjustability is limited to moving the door surface closer to or farther away from the vehicle's centerline (right or left). The door half of the hinge typically has the most adjustability, as the mounting holes in the hinge are slotted. This allows the door to be moved up or down, forward or backward, but not left or right. If you are lucky, the door-mounting bolts may just have come slightly loose and the door moved slightly during impact. This will allow you to loosen the mounting bolts a bit more, adjust the door to its proper position, and then retighten the bolts.

Before attempting to align a door, you should always check the hinge pin and bushing. If there is any slop, the hinge pin and/or bushing should be replaced, as you will not be able to properly align the door otherwise.

If any of the door hinges are obviously damaged, you are better off replacing the hinge, rather than attempting a repair. What may seem like a minor misalignment at the hinge will be more pronounced at the opposite end of the door.

Latches and Actuators

If an exterior door latch is damaged, you will most likely need to remove the interior door panel to gain access to the bolt that secures the latch. However, prior to completely removing the latch from the door after removing the mounting hardware, you will need to disconnect the actuator rods or linkage. Unless the method of reassembly is obvious beyond a doubt, make some detailed notes or take some photos to aid in reassembly, as a less-than-perfect reassembly will mar the repair and be noticeable every time you get in or out of the vehicle.

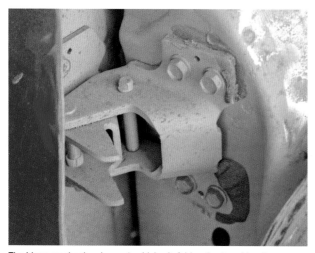

The hinge mechanism in most vehicles is fairly robust, making them reasonably durable during a collision. However, collision or rust damage to the cowl or B-pillar in a four-door sedan may require removal and reinstallation. This upper hinge simply bolts onto the cowl and the door, while newer versions are welded in place, requiring hinge pin removal to remove the door.

When you are in the process of disassembling a vehicle in preparation for making repairs, you may have to make some educated guesses about how things come apart. Most door handles attach from the inside, meaning that the interior door panel must be removed.

This lower hinge is comparable to the upper, except that it also includes a very stiff spring. The spring and the notched arm to which it mounts are here to hold the door open in one of two positions. If not for this spring mechanism, the door would fly open all the way (or stay closed) when unlatched while the vehicle is parked on a hill or incline.

With the exterior door handle already off, we can see that it attaches with two mounting screws from the inside. Whenever repairs are made to a door, it is best to remove the glass and door handles, then repaint the entire door, rather than painting just a portion. Even if no paint is applied to the door handle or glass area, removal and replacement is typically easier than masking these areas.

As actuators are relatively thin by design and span a large portion of the door's width, they are susceptible to impact damage any time a door is hit, especially if the door takes a direct hit. You will simply need to use your best judgment or rely on trial and error to see if you can repair (straighten) a damaged actuator rod well enough or purchase a new one. Although you will most likely need to purchase an entire door from your local salvage yard just to obtain the internal workings, the prudent course of action may be to replace and refinish (repaint) a good but usable door rather than attempting to repair one that has taken a direct hit.

Window Mechanisms

Among the items in the door that can be damaged, other key areas include the window glass, the window riser mechanism (manual or electric), and the window channel in which the glass slides. If they are damaged, these items are more likely to require replacement, rather than repair. Anything that may cause glass to be misaligned or in a bind will eventually lead it to break, so it is better to replace the necessary parts now while the vehicle is disassembled, instead of waiting until later, when you will have to disassemble and reassemble the door again.

PANEL REPLACEMENT

If the body damage is more severe than you can repair, or if you have hammered the affected panel into oblivion while attempting to straighten it, you may need to replace the damaged panel. As long as the original panel can be removed from the vehicle, this is always an option. Even a roof or quarter panel can be cut from a donor car and welded in place, if necessary.

If it is not obvious how to remove a damaged panel from your vehicle, you may be forced to do as professional body men do and simply begin taking off bolts until the panel can be removed. Information on how to do this for your vehicle may be available in a specific repair manual, but body panel removal information is usually not included in such books. As you remove the panel, make notes regarding the number and type of fasteners that are removed so that you can verify that the replacement panel is reinstalled and secured correctly. Also, take notes of any panels that overlap, should they need to be removed and reinstalled in a specific order.

Any subassemblies connected to the part being replaced are usually sold separately and therefore should be removed from the original and reused if possible. If these additional parts are not usable, they will need to

be replaced as well. Don't discard any panels that are being replaced until after all the repairs are made and the project is finished. Otherwise, you may be required to purchase a new widget or other seemingly insignificant component that is not included but turns out to be vital for reinstallation. The replaced parts can also serve as a visual reference for how the replacement parts should fit together.

Clean the replacement panels with wax and grease remover prior to doing anything else, then scuff the surface with 240-grit sandpaper so that primers and top coats adhere properly. Consult your auto paint supplier for any recommendations they may have concerning the correct undercoat for prepping the panels for the paint system you are using. Primer undercoats should be applied prior to the panel being installed on the vehicle. To allow for proper paint blending, top coats should be applied only after the panel has been installed and aligned. However, some panels, such as doors and hoods, may need to be painted (at least on the edges) before installation. Some of these areas are difficult to paint after installation and will stick out like the proverbial sore thumb if not painted. Painting will be discussed in detail in Chapter 9.

PANEL ALIGNMENT

Just because you have straightened every dent, removed every ripple, and have repaired (or replaced) all of the damaged panels, your work as a body man isn't finished. Before applying paint, you still need to make sure that all of these panels fit together as they should. Most obviously, all of the bodylines should align from one panel to the next. If any of these lines don't flow from one panel to the other, you will notice it immediately, as will others. Not so obvious, from a distance, but just as noticeable up close are the fits of each edge to its adjacent panel. Some vehicles fit better from the factory than others. How well they fit after you have painted the vehicle is up to you, though. If you can do this correctly, it will be a great testimony to your attention to detail.

You may need to install shims behind some panels to get them to align properly with adjacent panels, whether or not shims were used at the factory. Hoods and deck lids may present the biggest problem, as any ill fit will need to be split evenly between the two sides. Doors and fenders should be fit as accurately as possible, though slight variations from one side to the other will not be as noticeable as a hood or deck lid that is biased on one side.

continued on page 83

Even though this truck tailgate is going to be replaced with a new one, that new tailgate doesn't include the latch mechanism, linkage, or other hardware. This latch mechanism will not be seen after the access panel is reinstalled, so if the latch works and is not damaged cosmetically on the outside, you can save some money by using the old one, rather than replacing it.

This latch and the cable on each end will also be preserved. In this case, disassembly is rather straightforward. Any time you are replacing panels (especially doors, tailgates, hood, or deck lids), it is a good idea to leave the original hardware attached to the panel being replaced until you are ready to install it or replacement pieces on the new panel.

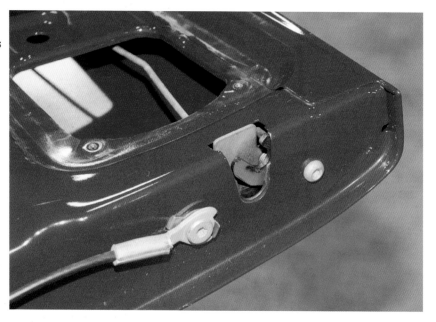

An air ratchet or drill makes quick work of removing or reinstalling fasteners used to hold body panels and their hardware together, but hand tools are less expensive.

Whenever you are working with linkages or anything that is similar but different from one side or the other, make sure that you label it. A little time spent labeling will be much easier than installing the piece in the wrong place and being required to disassemble and reinstall it later.

Seeing the big picture of the damage makes planning your repair strategy much easier, or at least you'll have a better idea of what needs to be done. On this Buick sedan, the right front wheel and tire assembly were pushed backward, causing the front fender to also move toward the rear.

The lower portion of the fender between the wheel opening and the door was pushed back more than at the top. This, in turn, pushed the door back at the bottom, causing the door to essentially rotate clockwise.

As the door rotated clockwise, its position is higher than it should be at the back. To properly align the door, the lower hinge will require work to move it back into correct position. When the hinge has been reworked, the door will fit and operate properly.

continued from page 79

Consistency in gap width is the prime objective, while factory tolerances or tighter will make for a good target. To obtain consistent gaps, you may be required to remove or add material to a panel. Although it is not always possible to meet this goal, body men commonly look for gaps the thickness of a paint stir stick.

If a panel is removed from the vehicle to make repairs, it should be reinstalled on the vehicle prior to adding any body filler; this will help verify that the body filler will not cause panel alignment problems. Any panels where body filler has been applied are suspect when gaps are too tight, since getting the surface smooth may have required too much buildup. This usually happens when a portion of the area being filled was actually higher than it should have been and the surrounding area is brought out to an incorrect surface height.

LIGHTS

Whenever a vehicle is in a collision, you should verify two things afterward: do the lights still function, and do the lenses require replacement. These are admittedly low-priority concerns in the big scheme of things, but you don't want to find out that your headlights don't work when you are driving at night and are away from home. Verifying that the lights work is easy to do: simply start the vehicle, check the turn signals, the headlights (high beam and low beam), and the brake lights. Check the lights at both the front and back of the vehicle. Having someone on hand to check with you will save you a few laps around the vehicle, but you can do this by yourself, too. To check the brake lights by yourself, back toward a vertical surface, stopping a foot or two away from it. With the vehicle stopped, keep your foot on the brake pedal and look in your inside rearview mirror. Unless there is an abundance of ambient light, you should be able to see the reflection or glow from the brake lights on the vertical surface. If not, the brake lights may not be working or you simply can't see them. In this case, enlist the help of a second person to verify that they are working.

For any lights that don't work, first check to make sure that the bulb is fully plugged in, as it may have been jarred loose in the accident. Then check to see if the bulb is burned out (it may have some discoloration) or broken, and replace if necessary. If these checks do not provide a reason for malfunction, check the appropriate fuse to see if it has blown. If so, replace it with the appropriate size fuse.

If none of these actions correct the problem, you most likely have a wiring problem. This could be a broken wire, a damaged light socket, or a ground wire may have come loose from its grounding connection.

If any of the light lenses are cracked or broken, replace them, as they cannot be repaired. You can purchase new lenses at a car dealer, some auto parts stores, or from a salvage yard. Prices will vary, so you decide between finding what you need or paying a little more and taking it home today.

Headlights

Many vehicles have headlight systems that turn the lights on automatically based upon ambient light. If your vehicle is equipped with this type of headlight switch, you may need to turn the switch on to the manual setting to verify that the headlights actually work.

Correct aiming is another concern with headlights. This is not as important on newer vehicles that have a replaceable bulb installed in the back of the headlamp assembly. However, on vehicles that use sealed-beam headlights, they should be aimed as accurately as possible.

To check the aim of your headlights, you need between 35 and 40 feet of uniformly sloped driving area and a wall. The driving surface does not have to be level, so your driveway and garage door may work. Park your vehicle so that the headlights are from two to three feet from the wall and turn on the low beam headlights. With some tape that can be easily removed, outline the bright spots of each headlight on the wall. Now back the vehicle straight back so that the headlights are now about 25 feet away from the wall. If you turned them off, turn the low beam headlights on again. The top of the low beam shining on the wall should be no higher than the top marks on the wall or lower than the center of the original area. Adjust as necessary and repeat the aiming process until it is dialed in.

BUMPERS

By design, bumpers should take the brunt of most damage in a vehicle collision. Sometimes they do, sometimes they don't, but that is beside the point. Your concern is how to repair or replace one if the bumper on your vehicle is damaged. Whether your bumper is chrome-plated or painted will have a direct impact (pun fully intended) on the method of repair.

Bumper Removal

When removing a bumper, you may need to use some spray lubricant, a long breaker bar, and/or an impact wrench to loosen the mounting hardware. Since the bumper hardware is usually exposed to the elements,

continued on page 97

HOW TO REPLACE A DOOR SKIN

To see how an old door skin is removed and a replacement installed, I visited Morfab Customs, where Chris was in the process of reskinning an early Camaro door. The process sounds more difficult than it actually is, and it's often a much better method for repairing a damaged door.

At the time of this writing, a replacement door skin for this vehicle costs about $100, while a replacement door costs around five times that much from the same source. Since in this case the repair must be made because of rust-through (due to some past amateur bodywork), installing a replacement door skin is the best course of action.

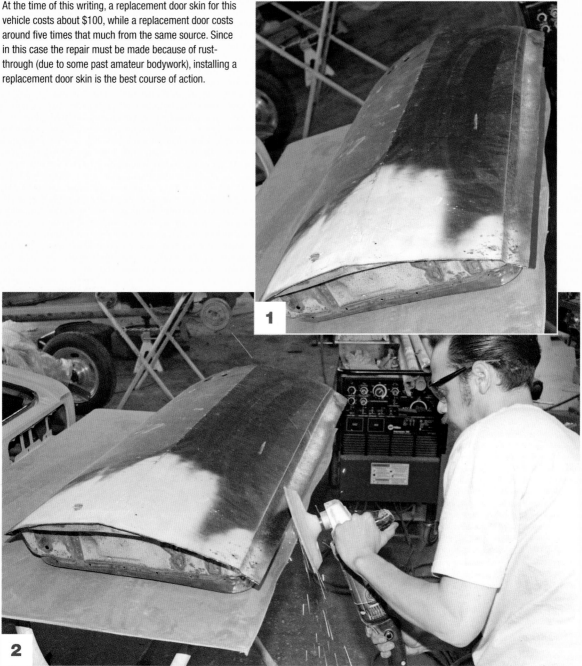

To remove a door skin, use a grinder with a 36- or 80-grit disc to grind through the edge of the door skin. Don't grind the face of the door or the flap that is folded over, only the very edge. This will quickly separate the skin from the door.

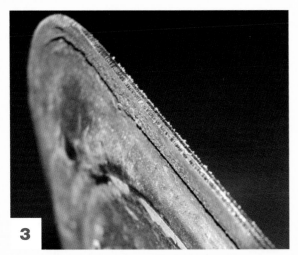

3

With the door skin separated at the door's edge, the skin can be removed from the outside of the door and the flap can be removed from the inside of the inner door panel. It may be necessary to drill out spot welds from some doors to remove the skin. With the door skin separated at the edge, the skin is now ready to be removed.

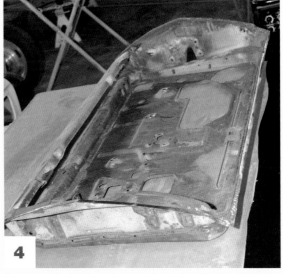

4

If you are so inclined, now is a good time to have the inner door panel media blasted or chemically dipped to remove any rust, and then follow up with a coat of epoxy primer. This door is solid, but lots of surface rust is apparent in the photo. The only time that you can effectively do any surface treatment to the inside of the door is between removing the skin and replacing it.

5

The replacement skin will be glued in place, then the edges of the skin will be wrapped around the inner panel, much as the original manufacture was done. In order for the glue to form a good bond, the mating area of the inner panel is scuffed with an angle head grinder to remove any paint or rust.

(continued)

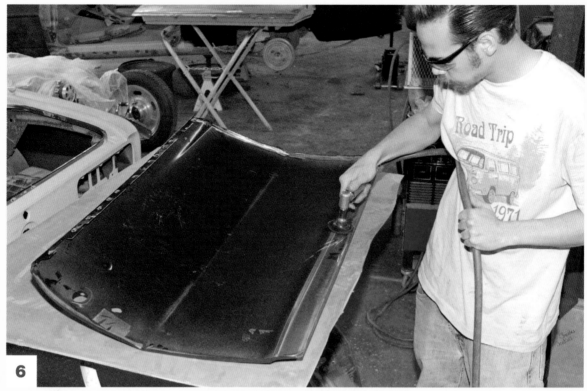

6

The mating surface of the replacement skin is scuffed in similar fashion. The original doors did not use glue to attach the door skins, but it does make for a better repair.

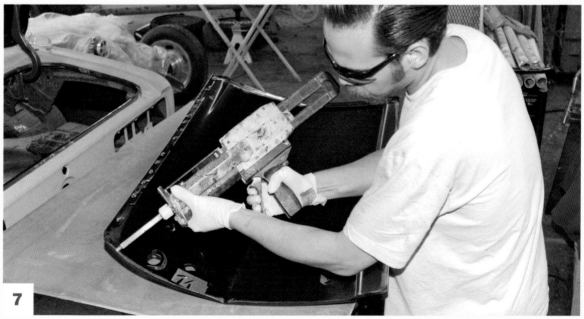

7

The glue used for securing a door skin is 3M's Door Skin Adhesive, a two-part epoxy that does require a specialized application gun that mixes the two parts as they are dispensed. Since the two parts are not mixed until they are used, the product has a longer shelf life.

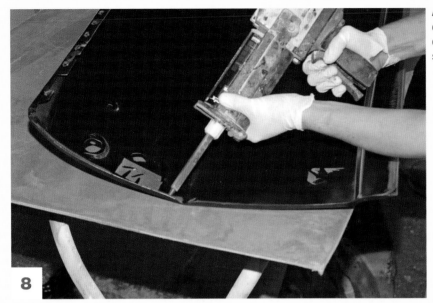

Application guns are used much like a caulking gun. Chris begins at the top of one side of the replacement door skin, working his way down that side.

Chris then continues across the bottom of the door skin, all the time making sure that the adhesive is applied to the surface that will abut the inner panel.

(continued)

A bead approximately a quarter-inch wide is basically centered on the door skin where the surface has already been scuffed.

Chris continues to apply the adhesive to the top of the door, opposite from where he started. The lip that does not have any adhesive applied actually fits over a portion of the inner door panel.

To avoid contaminating the adhesive with oils from his fingertips, Chris puts on a disposable glove, then uses his fingertips to spread the adhesive.

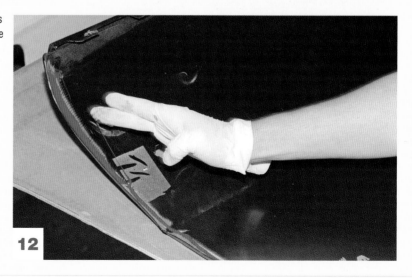

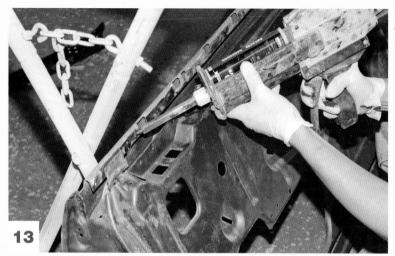

Chris then applies a bit of adhesive on the lip of the inner door panel where the outer door skin will lap over.

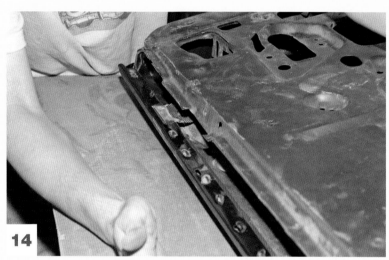

With the door skin exterior-side down and sitting on a suitable work surface, the inner door panel is slid into place. Make sure that the inner door panel is positioned as far into the door skin as possible, and is centered front-to-back.

The previous steps are not required if you aren't using adhesive to secure the door. With the door skin and the inner door panel adequately positioned in relation to each other, the tedious portion of the repair begins: hammering the edges of the outer door skin over the edge and flat.

(continued)

At this point, portions of the door skin are at about 90 degrees to the flange that they will be hammered over, while at other areas the skin is at about 180 degrees.

Before hammering any of the edge over the flange, the door skin should be clamped in place with as many clamps as you have available. You definitely do not want the door skin moving in relation to the inner door panel. The adhesive is still pliable at this time.

At a minimum, try to clamp the door skin to the inner panel at the four corners. You may have to move some of the clamps while hammering, so having multiple clamps in use will help prevent movement between the two panels.

Besides preventing movement between the two panels, the clamps hold the two pieces together tighter, allowing you to fold the edge over tighter and provide a better seam.

Chris will use a hammer-on dolly approach for folding the door skin edge over the inner door panel flange. In other words, he will hammer directly onto the dolly, with the two panels in between the tools.

To minimize marring of the new door skin, Chris has wrapped a shop towel tightly around the dolly. When skinning a door, you don't want the dolly to have any effect on the door skin, but the dolly is required so that the hammer doesn't bounce off the door panels. The shop towel provides some padding to prevent marring, but still provides a solid surface to hammer against.

(continued)

Chris works his way around the door skin, hammering the edge over slightly with each pass. You should avoid completely hammering the door skin edge over all at once.

Notice that Chris' hammer has one end that is straight and another that is curved. This curved end allows the user to strike the surface at a perpendicular angle when in tight situations.

The curved end may also be useful where there is ample room, but when the work piece and the body man are positioned at an angle, working with the straight end of the hammer may require extra effort.

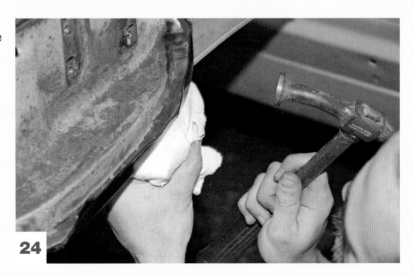

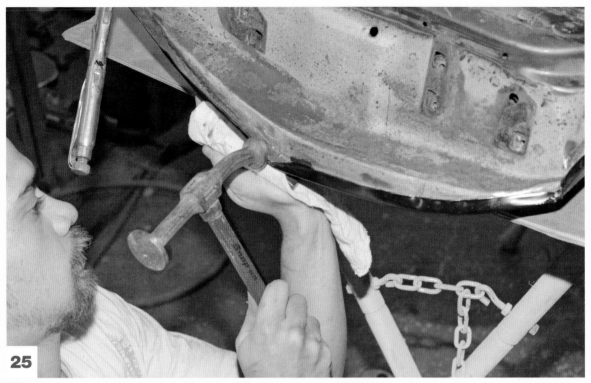

25

With each pass around the door, the skin is folded over a little more.

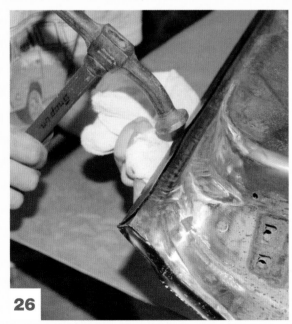

26

In this photo, the edge of the door skin is clearly closer to being flat and flush with the inner door panel. To avoid damage to the door skin, several relatively light taps are more productive than fewer, heavier hits. One of the secrets to successful body work and metal working in general is practicing finesse.

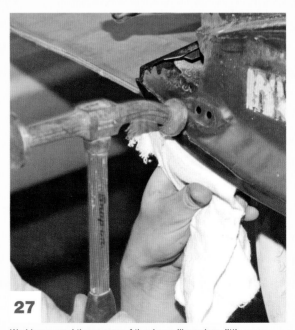

27

Working around the corners of the door will require a little more effort to get the desired result.

(continued)

HOW TO REPLACE A DOOR SKIN *(CONTINUED)*

Chris keeps the shop towel tightly wrapped around the dolly to help minimize damage to the outside of the door skin.

28

Special attention will be required where the door changes shape. Take your time, use finesse, and you will learn how to maneuver through these areas like a pro.

29

Take your time to make sure that the door skin edge is hammered as flat as possible against the inside of the inner door panel. If it is not flat, it won't look right.

30

31

Coming down the back stretch, this door skin installation is almost finished. Chris has installed lots of door skins, but the process still takes about an hour. It will most likely take longer for a novice.

32

After all of the hammering has been completed, install as many clamps as possible so that the adhesive cures evenly. The 3M Door Skin Adhesive will require about four hours to cure completely.

(continued)

33 Virtually as good as a new door, but considerably less expensive, this door requires normal paint preparation at this point.

34 This is the door for the opposite side of the vehicle. Chris had reskinned it earlier in the day—no dents, no rust, and almost ready for paint.

COLLISION REPAIR: METAL

continued from page 83

it is among the first to corrode and rust. Use a floor jack or enlist the aid of a helper to support the bumper as you remove the last bolts and set it aside. After the bumper bolts are removed, verify that none of the bolts are bent, stripped, or otherwise damaged. If they are, replace them before you reinstall the original or replacement bumper.

Bumper Brackets

After the bumper has been removed, verify that the bumper brackets are not damaged and that the hardware securing them to the vehicle's chassis is still tight. If any of the brackets are damaged, they will need to be straightened or replaced, then remounted to the vehicle. You should also verify that no mounting bolts have been sheared off. If they have, they will require replacement.

Bumper Repair

Any straightening method will most likely damage the bumper's chrome plating. You can hammer on the bumper in an effort to straighten it out and then have it re-chromed. Since the bumper is usually composed of heavy-duty metal, it isn't as easy to straighten as body-grade sheet metal. Additionally, if the bumper is to be re-chromed, no conventional body filler can be used, as it would not withstand the temperature that is required during the chroming process. Even though chrome plating is something you could do at home, as I have discussed in my book, *How To Plate, Polish and Chrome,* having a tank large enough for a bumper usually is not feasible for the hobbyist. Re-chroming a bumper that has been damaged will probably cost more than buying a new bumper. When you figure in the time spent straightening and the cost for re-chroming, buying a replacement bumper will most likely be your best option.

If the bumper is painted, rather than plated, you can do a certain amount of bodywork on it, just as if it were another piece of sheet metal. Again, "it's gonna take a bigger hammer," as it is heavier material, but you can use body filler to smooth the surface before priming and painting.

Bumper Replacement

Whether the bumper is a replacement or has been refinished, reassembly is straightforward. Enlist an assistant to help you set the bumper into position and insert all of the bolts through the bumper and bumper brackets. Install a large washer over each bolt after they have passed through the bumper bracket and then install a lockwasher and nut, or a self-locking nut. Hand-tighten the nuts and then verify that the bumper is centered side-to-side and sits level with the vehicle. When the bumper is positioned correctly, tighten all of the nuts with an appropriately sized wrench or socket.

COLLISION REPAIR: METAL

Seeing the big picture of the damage makes planning your repair strategy much easier, or at least you'll have a better idea of what needs to be done. On this Buick sedan, the right front wheel and tire assembly were pushed backward, causing the front fender to also move toward the rear.

Chapter 6
Collision Repair: Composites

There are many different kinds of plastics in use today for all types of automobile parts and assemblies. They range from acrylonitrile butadiene styrene (ABS) and thermoplastic olefin (TPO) to sheet molding compounds (SMC) and reaction injection molded plastic (RIM). Each has its own place, from rigid grillework sections to flexible bumper covers.

This use of plastics (composites) in automobiles has changed the auto body repair business substantially. On the positive side, composites don't rust and are generally lighter weight than similar panels made of sheet metal. These are two distinct advantages for the automobile manufacturers, as they indirectly have a positive effect on their sales. Put simply, composites don't rust and lighter vehicles don't burn as much fuel. Eliminating rust and increasing corporate fuel averages is big business.

On the negative side, because of their chemical makeup, plastic-based composites are either brittle or flexible. Brittle composites, such as those used in many fenders, quarter panels, and door skins, will crack and break when impacted. Flexible composites, such as those used in bumper/fascia assemblies, will withstand a certain amount of impact, but they won't rebound once they are pushed beyond their elastic range.

Overall, newer vehicles are designed for composite body panels to absorb most of the impact forces that occur in a collision. The substructure of these vehicles also absorbs shock throughout the vehicle's crumple zones. Overall, these design changes provide greater occupant safety when involved in a collision, which is certainly a good thing. However, the vehicle involved in what seemed like a minor accident, which you were able to walk away from, is probably totaled, or at least it's damaged beyond the simple repair a hobbyist can perform. Still, the hobbyist can make some repairs to these composite panels.

BASIC CRACK REPAIR

Whether the damaged composite panel is rigid or flexible, it is susceptible to cracks upon impact. As long as the affected panel is still partially connected or can be clamped back together in the correct shape, it can be repaired rather easily by using a panel adhesive designed for composite automobile panels. Removing the panel to gain better access to the backside will be beneficial.

First clean the back of the panel with wax and grease remover to prevent contaminants from being trapped beneath the panel adhesive. Then use a small grinder to scuff up the surface and promote adhesion. You should also use the grinder to cut a slight "V" groove along the crack to provide more surface area for the adhesive. Cut a piece of 3M Duramix structural gauze to a size that will cover the crack to be filled, then saturate the structural gauze with 3M Duramix adhesive (generically known as panel bond or panel adhesive). Press the gauze into place, using a body filler spreader to work out any bubbles. After the adhesive becomes tacky, apply another piece of saturated structural gauze to increase the strength of the repaired area.

After the crack is patched from the backside and the panel adhesive is dry to the touch, you can go about cosmetic repair to the outside. Use some 36-grit sandpaper by hand or on a sanding disc to scuff the outside surface and then clean it with wax and grease remover. Mix an appropriate amount of plastic body filler and hardener, then use a spreader to press the filler into the crack and onto the surrounding area. As the filler begins to get tacky, begin sanding it with 80- or 100-grit sandpaper to remove the excess filler, then smooth it with 180- or 220-grit sandpaper. Apply additional filler if necessary and sand as much as it takes to match the surrounding surface in both shape and texture.

PANEL REPAIR/REPLACEMENT

If the panel has damage larger than a crack, it can still be repaired as long as you can connect enough pieces together and you have access to the backside. In much the same way as completing a puzzle, having all of the necessary pieces will make the task easier. As long as you can fit enough pieces together to recreate the outline and the contour of the panel, it can be repaired by using panel adhesive and structural gauze. This procedure is fundamentally the same as that used in fixing a crack, described above. The big difference is that you may be required to use cardboard or masking tape to form up the front side of the surface being repaired, preventing the panel adhesive from sinking too far forward; if not done correctly, this can result in a high spot when viewed from the outside. When the original damaged panel is repaired or a replacement panel has been prepped for paint, it can be reinstalled on the vehicle and painted using conventional paint procedures.

Contemporary bumpers are considerably different from those "5 mph bumpers" from 1980s and 1990s vehicles and are significantly different from bumpers of vehicles that are even older. The former typically had a tube in an arrangement attaching the bumper to the vehicle's chassis, while the latter had formed metal brackets bolted to the bumper and the chassis. The white portion of this bumper is actually a piece of molded foam that covers a piece of alloy tubing that spans the front of the vehicle and is hidden when the bumper/fascia is in place.

Today's flexible bumper/fascia assemblies typically slide into grooves, tracks, or clips on the fender for alignment purposes. The bumper/fascia is then secured to the fender with a number of screws or bolts that are usually installed from the inside of the wheelwell. This virtually eliminates all fasteners from view when looking at the bumper/fascia assembly.

To align the bumper/fascia assembly on the vehicle, the two notches shown near the top edge (toward upper left of photo) slide onto mating buttons on the fender. Bolts, screws, or other types of fasteners pass through the lower fender extension and into the mounting flange shown at the far left of the photo. Most likely, another fastener is used at the protrusion located on the top edge, adjacent to the headlight or taillight. While this is a front assembly, the rear would attach in similar fashion.

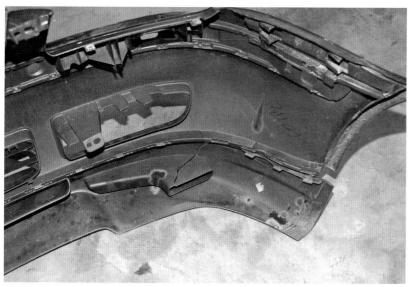

This panel was replaced rather than repaired, though it could be repaired if desired. Other than cosmetic damage that can be easily repaired, some structural damage would need to be repaired as well. In the bodyline located about a third of the way up from the bottom, the bumper/fascia has a crack or tear that runs partially around a curve and then down across the air duct. By clamping the separated pieces back together and then applying 3M Duramix urethane adhesive and Duramix structural gauze, the assembly can be repaired.

HOW TO REPLACE GLASS

If you are merely repainting a vehicle or one section, you don't need to remove the window glass as long as you can mask it properly. However, when faced with collision repair, it will often be necessary to remove the glass for a variety of reasons. The main reason for removal will be to replace whatever glass has been cracked or broken. Even if the glass is unscathed in an accident, it may be easier to remove it and reinstall it later than to risk breaking it yourself during the repair process.

Since paint should be cured by the time you begin installing glass, consider laying strips of wide masking tape along the window frame edges to guard against accidental bumps that could otherwise cause paint scratches or nicks. Be sure to use automotive masking tape, as generic tape might leave adhesive residue on surfaces. Whether you are replacing window glass out of necessity or convenience, installing glass after a vehicle body has been painted must be done with care in order to avoid scratches or nicks along the edges of the window frame. Even the smallest paint chip could allow an oxidation process to begin. Once started, especially on areas hidden by trim, oxidation will spread under layers of paint and not be noticed until severe metal rust damage causes paint finishes to bubble, crack, or otherwise present noticeable problems. Should that occur, repair efforts may require extensive metal work and new paint.

Along with recognizing the importance of preventing paint chips while installing glass, you should be concerned about watertight seals all around window perimeters. Not only are water leaks annoying, they can lead to corrosion damage on metal panels and rot or mildew in upholstery and carpeting.

Window glass is held in place in different ways, and not all makes and models use identical attachment methods. Some may feature clips, others rely on thick rubber molding, and many call for strips of butyl- or urethane-based sealers to hold panels safely in place. If you are not familiar with auto glass installation, consider hiring a professional to complete the work for you. Most auto glass businesses offer mobile service, allowing specialists to complete glass installations, or removals, at your working location.

Rear window glass on older model pickup trucks and hatchbacks is often set inside grooves along the inside perimeter of heavy rubber moldings. Another groove is set around the outer molding perimeter. Once the molding is fitted around glass, a cord is inserted into the outer perimeter groove and pulled taut. While one person holds the glass and molding unit in place from outside the vehicle, another person starts pulling the cord from inside the vehicle.

The combination of outside force being put on the glass or molding unit against a window opening and a person on the inside pulling out the cord causes the

continued on page 105

HOW TO REINSTALL A BUMPER/FASCIA ASSEMBLY

By using composite materials and wraparound design, the bumper/fascia assembly on contemporary vehicles absorbs much of the force that occurs in a front-end or rear-end automobile collision. By absorbing much of this force, there is typically less damage to the sheet metal around the main passenger compartment, and far fewer passenger injuries.

Even if the bumper/fascia assembly remains intact, as in a side impact, it will most likely need to be removed and reinstalled to gain access to the damaged panels. To see how to reinstall one of these composite bumper/fascia assemblies, follow along as the crew at Jerry's Auto Body finishes the repair on a common SUV.

1

Now that all of the bodywork and painting have been completed, it is time to begin reassembling the various pieces and parts that have been removed from the vehicle. All vehicles may differ somewhat, but the basic procedure for installing a bumper/fascia assembly is much the same for front or back.

2

Composite bumper/fascia assemblies are light enough to pick up by yourself, but will require a second set of hands to reinstall properly. As seen in this photo, when unassembled, it will have a great amount of flexibility. Trying to install one by yourself would most likely lead to scratched or chipped paint, something you don't want.

3

Typically, there are aligned grooves or tracks in the bumper/fascia assembly and the body. Make sure that the bumper/fascia is aligned properly and then slide it toward the body until it is in the correct position.

(continued)

COLLISION REPAIR: COMPOSITES

4

On this particular model, and presumably others, the bumper/fascia slides over an alignment track and then "snaps" into the correct position. To get the assembly to "snap," you may need to apply a little bit of force, such as from the open palm of your hand to fully seat the assembly.

5

The bumper/fascia assembly is secured in place by several screws through the body at the wheel opening and into the front edge of the bumper/fascia assembly.

6

Start all of the fasteners by hand, making sure that everything is aligned properly. Then the fasteners can be tightened until they are snug, but not so tight that they might pull through the bodywork.

continued from page 101

inside portion of the molding's outer perimeter to fold over a sheet metal body lip around the center of the vehicle's window opening. Both installers have to communicate and work together in order to complete this task. The easiest results have been found when the bottom sections of molding units are placed first, followed by alternately inching along the sides and finally completing the top by pulling from each outer end toward the middle.

Installation of fixed-glass units with urethane sealer actually adds a degree of structural strength to some automobiles. Windshields and side-mounted, fixed-glass units on newer cars and vans are commonly secured in place by continuous beads of urethane sealer. In some cases, a bead of butyl material is used instead of urethane. Butyl has a strength of approximately 5 psi, while urethane boasts adhesion strength of approximately 500 psi.

Instances that call for butyl beads alone are usually those where extensive bodywork was completed at or near window openings. Concerns over possible imperfect body window openings and resultant water leaks may require glass removal so that body sheet metal adjustments can be made. Since butyl is not nearly as strong as urethane, the removal of such glass units is much easier.

About the only way to remove fixed-glass units secured by butyl or urethane beads is to actually cut through the beads with a special tool. Essentially, the tool consists of a piece of strong wire with handles on each end; it requires two people to operate. An opening is made in the urethane bead and the wire is then inserted through it. With handles then attached at both ends, a person on the inside and another on the outside maneuver the wire around the fixed glass to cut through the urethane bead. Afterward, a special solvent is used to loosen old bead material for its removal.

The installation of fixed-glass units requires that their supportive body opening be clean from all contaminants. Then, a bead of butyl material is laid around the perimeter of the window opening. For butyl-only installations, the bead is solidly shaped. If urethane will also be used, the butyl bead's side that touches the vehicle body will be angled at about 45 degrees. Along that angle, urethane material will be placed to fill in the triangular void left open by the butyl bead's 45 degree angle.

For either kind of installation, butyl actually holds glass in place. This is an important factor for urethane jobs, as it takes some time for the material to cure

fully. While it is curing, butyl holds the glass in a fixed position. The end result should be a near-perfect and leak-free installation.

The tools and materials needed to remove and install fixed-glass units are available at auto body paint and supply stores. Be sure that you fully understand all installation instructions for the products you use. In addition, have a helper available to assist you in removing or replacing glass units, as they can be quite heavy and cumbersome.

How to Replace a Windshield

There are basically two types of windows in an automobile: fixed glass and opening glass. Fixed glass is used in windows that do not open, such as the windshield, back window, and rear quarter windows. Glass from fixed windows is taken out by first removing any trim around the window seal, removing the rubber by using a special tool designed for this task, then pushing the window glass outward. Any residual window caulk or sealant must be removed from the sheet metal around the window opening. Some of these windows are glued in place, while others are held in place by rubber weather strip. For the type that is glued in place, the sheet metal window opening must be free of debris or broken glass and clean and free of contaminants; this can be ensured by cleaning with wax and grease remover, then applying the glue to the flange in the window opening. The glass is then set into position and pressed into place to ensure full contact with the glue. Leave the vehicle for the proper amount of time for the glue to set.

For glass that is secured by weather strip, as with the glued-in type, the sheet metal window opening must be clean. The rubber weather strip is stretched around the window glass, making sure that the weather strip is properly oriented around the glass. Spray silicone is then applied to the inside lip of the weather strip and a thin cord or rope (about ⅛ inch in diameter) is slid into the lip that fits around the flange in the window opening. The cord or rope should overlap at the top or bottom of the glass so that it protrudes toward the inside of the vehicle long enough that you can hold opposite ends of the rope in each hand. With the help of an assistant, the glass and weather strip is set in place outside the vehicle. By pulling the rope inward (out of the weather strip), the weather strip can pass over the window opening flange. The cord or rope is pulled in slowly while the assistant outside of the vehicle pushes the glass in place.

HOW TO REINSTALL WEATHER STRIP AND DOOR GLASS

Any time a door is damaged, the glass and interior door panel should be removed to make the necessary repairs. The key here is finding out the way that the interior door panel is secured. In newer vehicles, the door panel often simply snaps into place, which means it can be pried off easily. However, there will usually be one or more screws located around the interior door latch mechanism, often inside the door pull and other "out-of-view" locations. With the interior door panel removed, you will now have access to the various bolts and screws that hold everything in place inside the door. When disassembling the door, make sure that you contain all hardware and make notes of anything that you may not remember when you get ready to reassemble the door.

Reassembling the door, its glass, and weather strip is typically the reverse of disassembly. Follow along as Mike at Jerry's Auto Body reinstalls these items on an SUV that has both fixed and opening glass in one door.

A piece of rubber weather strip that fits between the glass and all portions of the window frame is installed where a weather-tight seal is required. This particular door will have two pieces, since there are actually two pieces of glass. In this instance, a tall, skinny piece of glass is fixed in place, with a division bar adjacent to the front edge to provide a track for the opening section.

If you aren't sure how some of the pieces fit into place, refer to the other side of the vehicle, assuming it was not damaged. If both sides were damaged and therefore require disassembly, you may need to refer to the photos or notes that you took throughout the disassembly process.

Since this weather strip is made especially for this vehicle, the corners are molded in and therefore provide a hint as to how it fits into place. If you were using "universal" weather strip, this would not be so evident. Regardless of whether it is universal or model specific, the weather strip is pushed into the opening around the perimeter of the window opening.

3

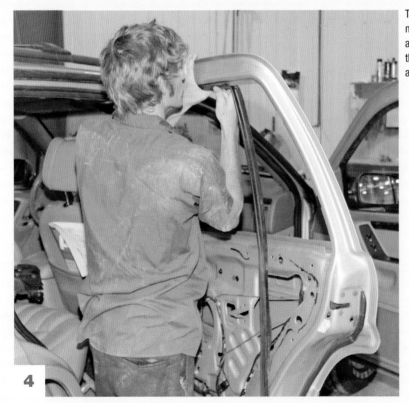

There may be notches in the door sheet metal that provide indications for the proper alignment of the weather strip. Just make sure that you get it aligned and seated properly to avoid leaks.

4

(continued)

HOW TO REINSTALL WEATHER STRIP AND DOOR GLASS *(CONTINUED)*

Since this Jeep has two pieces of glass in the door, along with a division bar, the operable glass is installed first. Installing the glass can be tricky, but the main thing to remember is to not get it in a bind, which will cause it to crack or break. Door glass will often have some slight curve to it, which will often necessitate installing the glass from the outside, as shown, or it may need to be slid in at an angle.

5

By looking through the access panel, you can see to align the bottom of the glass with its window track and riser mechanism. There will usually be some sort of clips, rather than nuts and bolts, to secure the glass to the riser. However, make sure that the glass is merely secure, not over tightened.

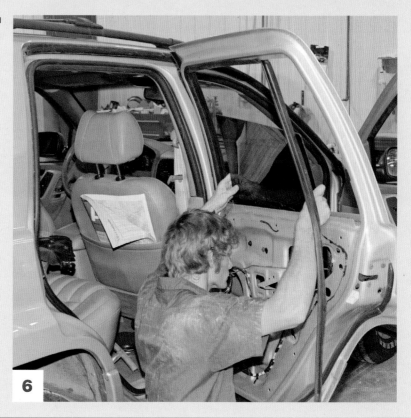

6

With the door glass installed, you should install the window crank mechanism or connect the power window switch and slowly run the glass through its up-and-down cycle a couple of times. If there is any binding, stop and correct the situation.

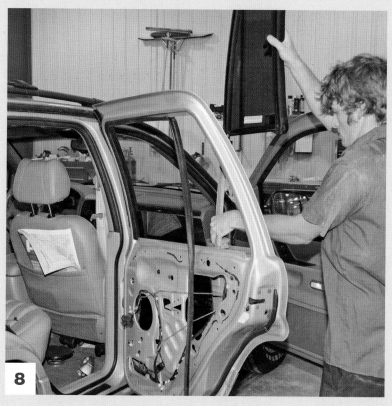

Now the fixed glass and its attached division bar can be installed. As seen here, the division bar is much longer than the glass, as it also serves as a track for the glass that moves. Carefully insert the division bar into the door opening and continue sliding it downward until it is in position. Be carefully not to catch any wires or door latch linkages.

(continued)

Do not use a hammer, but you may need to "bump" the division bar with your hand a few times to fully seat it in the opening.

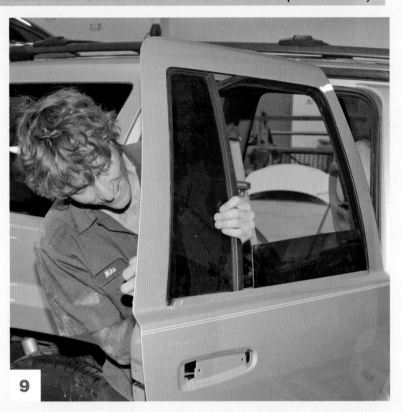

With the division bar installed, check and verify the correct operation of the opening glass again. If it doesn't work smoothly, find the problem and fix it. You will see in this photo that there is quite a gap between the opening glass and the division bar where the weather stripping has not yet been installed.

Almost forgot to install a screw at the top of the division bar—pull the weather strip down as required and install the screw.

Insert the loose end of the weather stripping into the door opening. Now press the weather strip into place around the top of the window opening and along the front edge of the division bar.

(continued)

The division bar will usually be secured to the door by one or two screws: do not forget to install these.

This particular vehicle secures the division bar at a total of three places. One is at the top of the window opening, the second is just below the bottom of the window opening, and the third is near the bottom of the division bar. Making sure that the division bar is secure will help to ensure that there is no binding in the operation of the window.

Chapter 7
Rust Repair

This salmon (pink) color on this firewall and cowl is weld-through primer. The primer provides short-term protection to the metal surface, but does not have to be ground away prior to doing any welding. When any welding is completed and prior to applying any body filler, primer, or paint, an application of epoxy primer should be applied.

Although we usually envision collision repair whenever we think of automotive bodywork, rust repair is often just as common. Rust may be rare in some regions, but it is all too common in the rest of the world. Anywhere that humidity meets unprotected sheet metal, rust is hard at work eating its way through your automobile's sheet metal. Sadly, you may not even know that rust is present, as it tends to do its damage to areas of your vehicle that you don't normally see during everyday operation. When dealing with rust, you should determine whether it is just surface rust or a rust-through.

If you find that it is surface rust, with solid metal beneath, you can deal with the rust by sanding and then applying an epoxy primer. If the rust is more severe, with either complete rust-through or severely pitted sheet metal, more extensive repairs are necessary before paint can be applied. This may necessitate media blasting or the use of a chemical stripper, along with the application of epoxy primer followed by a high-build primer-surfacer. It may be necessary to weld in patch panels if the rust is severe enough.

Note that an application of primer-surfacer or even epoxy primer alone will not prevent rust from reoccurring. The best defense against rust is proper application of paint to all metal surfaces, along with regular washing and applications of wax. Until paint is applied, an application of epoxy primer is the most effective rust deterrent. Simply applying primer-surfacer will not prevent rust, as primer-surfacer is actually porous and therefore soaks up moisture, the primary cause of rust.

A small patch panel has been fabricated in the shop, then welded in place to fill a stock opening in the firewall that will no longer be required. For this firewall or any flat areas, patch panels can easily be cut from 18- to 22-gauge sheet metal to fill any large holes.

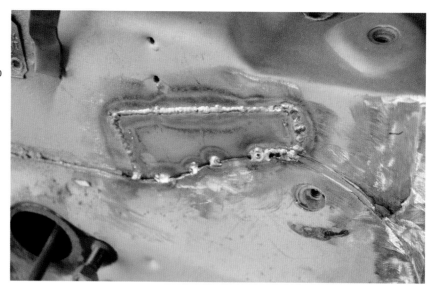

Special care must be taken any time you are doing bodywork on a convertible, especially if the doors are going to be removed. Since there is no upper body support provided by a roof, it is very likely that the weight of the body would cause it to pull away from itself if not adequately supported.

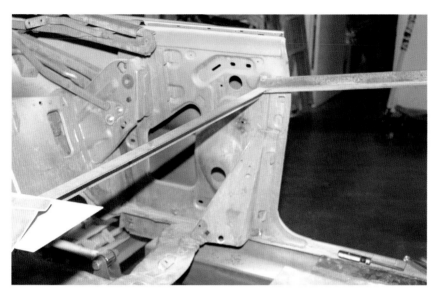

By temporarily tack welding some angle iron or electrical conduit between the cowl and the rear quarter panels front to back and between the quarter panels side to side, damage caused due to body flex can be minimized if not eliminated. The material used to brace must be suitably strong in both compression and tension.

PATCH PANELS

Patch panels have been used extensively on vintage restorations and hot rods, but their use is becoming more common on later model vehicles as the average vehicle age increases with more efficient designs. Patch panels differ from replacement panels, as they are typically just a portion of the entire panel. Common patch panels can be used to repair lower doors, portions of fenders, rocker panels, or cab corners on pickup trucks.

An ever-expanding restoration aftermarket provides more patch panels for vehicles every year. As more vehicles begin to show their rust-prone areas, more companies have taken to producing parts for repairing these areas. If a certain make and model vehicle begins to show a tendency to rust on the left side of the trunk floor, the aftermarket will work to fill this demand. This automotive aftermarket develops new products based largely on the laws of supply and demand, so if you have the only one of these vehicles that rusts on the right side, the panel may not be available. If you are working on a mainstream vehicle, chances are that the necessary patch panel for your particular application is available. Even if available patch panels are not big enough to cover the entire area to be repaired, one may be useful for repairing the intricate bodylines of the damaged area.

If the sheet metal has been media-blasted, chemically dipped, or stripped by some other method, the extent of the necessary rust repair will be fairly obvious. However, if the suspect panel still wears a coat of paint, you will need to do some investigating. Paint that appears to be bubbling up from the surface is most likely hiding rust beneath the surface. You can use a small screwdriver or ice pick to map out the extent of the rust. Begin by poking the screwdriver or ice pick into the middle of the suspected area: if it goes right through, you have a rust-through problem and should continue poking in small circles and growing outward around the center. When you begin hitting metal, where the screwdriver or ice pick will not go through, you are most likely hitting sheet metal that is still usable. However, there may be additional rust pockets located nearby.

After completing this probing to determine the extent of the rust, purchase a patch panel that will cover the entire area. Remember that not all patch panels will be large enough to cover all areas of rust. Before cutting away any of the area that will be removed, compare the patch panel with the area that is to be repaired. If possible, slip the panel roughly into place over the existing one and trace around the edge with a permanent marker; this will show the limits of what can be removed. However, don't simply cut at this line. You should mark a second line approximately an inch inside of this line and use it to indicate the area for removal. Now use a plasma cutter, die grinder, reciprocating saw, or tin snips to cut along this second line to remove the rusty panel. Prior to welding in any patch panels or replacement panels, confirm that the vehicle is supported properly. If the vehicle's body is twisted in any way and a new panel is welded in place, it will cause major panel alignment problems later on. Fit the new panel into place and check it for proper alignment, then clamp it into place and weld.

This lower door shows indications of prior damage that was repaired with body filler but never completely sanded, and then protected only with a coat or two of lacquer-based primer. The body filler never smoothed itself down and the primer did not provide adequate protection from the elements, resulting in rust-through.

The type of weld to use is largely dependent on the actual panel being replaced, the type of welder being used, and your welding skills. When welding with a MIG welder, start with ⅛-inch tacks and skip around to avoid getting the panel too hot, which can cause distortion. Another tip is to use your air hose with an air nozzle to blow cool air on the welds; this will keep them from getting too hot.

After all welding is completed, clean the patched area with wax and grease remover, then apply epoxy primer and finish bodywork to the surrounding area. Follow with primer-surfacer and block sanding as necessary prior to applying sealer and top coats.

continued on page 143

This is the opposite door of the same vehicle, with the same poor-quality repair. Although the rust-through is not as bad on this side, it could have been prevented by finishing the repair rather than just applying primer.

HOW TO REPLACE A PARTIAL QUARTER PANEL

To get the lowdown on installing a replacement quarter panel, I visited Morfab Customs where Brent Schmelz was working on an early Chevrolet Camaro. The original quarter panel had already been removed so that the new seam would be at the top bodyline where the quarter panel goes from horizontal to vertical. Using a plasma cutter, the original panel was cut away, but a reciprocating saw, die grinder, or sheet metal shears could have been used. The replacement quarter from Goodmark Industries was aligned and clamped into place at the tail panel, at the front of the panel at the door where the wheelwell aligns with the wheelhouse. Using a MIG welder, the new quarter panel was spot welded approximately every six inches, then seam welded for the entire length of the mating seam.

This is actually a different vehicle than in the following photos, but it is the same make and model and will be treated to the same panel replacement. For this particular vehicle, the replacement panel is designed to be welded on precisely at the bodyline that delineates the profile of the rear quarter panel.

After removing the original quarter panel, any loose crumbs of rust were removed from the inner structure. To prevent further rust formation, two coats of POR-15 were applied. The POR-15 should not be used as a topcoat, though it is designed to "paint over rust" in an effort to protect areas that never received any protective coating from the factory.

(continued)

RUST REPAIR

The quarter panel should be stitch welded around the perimeter when it is installed. Note that the trapezoid-shaped sheet metal panel above the wheelhouse should be plug welded to the top of the wheelhouse. Either this vehicle has been repaired incorrectly before or the welding was not completed at the factory. Evidence such as this should be a clue that you should double check everything when aligning panels, as some things may not be correct.

3

The original quarter panel has been removed and the replacement panel installed. It was aligned, tack welded in place, double-checked to verify proper alignment, and then stitch welded along the entire seam.

4

The light gray area is the portion of the replacement quarter panel that has been scuffed up prior to welding, while the black area is the primer applied to the replacement panel by the manufacturer. With the high quality of stitch welds securing the quarter panel in place, the weld itself is difficult to see, even from close up.

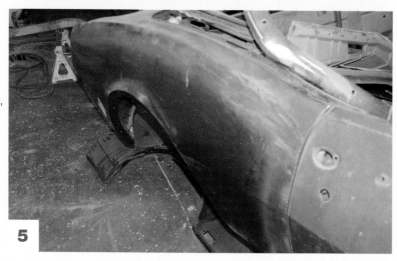

5

RUST REPAIR

6 Still, the welds should be ground down so that they are flush with the body or slightly below. By using an angle head die grinder and a 36-grit disc, Brent makes reasonably quick work of this.

7 Any time you are using a grinder, please wear eye protection to save your eyesight. Brent also should be wearing long sleeves and a face mask.

8 Install the interior garnish molding at the bottom of the window. On newer vehicles, this will generally snap into place, but it might be secured with trim screws on older vehicles.

9 You must take the time to grind the welds in the intricate areas as well. Bodywork consists of doing layers of tasks, so each one must be completed as accurately and completely as possible, or it will have a negative impact on the tasks that follow.

(continued)

10

After an initial pass, Brent checks to verify that he did not miss any welds. Finding some that are still a little high, he hits them with a grinder again.

11

From this perspective, you can gain a better idea of where the partial quarter panel is attached to the body, along with how much area should be ground smooth.

12

Even though this is a new replacement panel, it is not perfect, so it will need a skim coat of filler. For the filler to adhere properly, a DA orbital sander with 80- to 100-grit sandpaper is used to scuff the surface.

RUST REPAIR

Fiberglass-reinforced body filler should always be used as the first filler over areas that have been welded, such as replacement or patch panels. This will greatly improve adhesion of additional materials. It is also highly recommended for areas that are prone to rust.

13

14

A plastic cutting board such as one that would be used in the kitchen makes a perfect surface for mixing body filler. They are inexpensive, very durable, and clean up easily. Whatever you use as a palette, pour or scoop the desired amount of filler onto the middle of it.

15

Squeeze the recommended amount of hardener onto the filler. The correct amount of hardener will become more familiar as you work through the project, but it will be a trial-and-error process when you begin. Typically, a proportionate amount of hardener is used with the filler (in other words, ¼ of the hardener should be used with ¼ of the filler).

16

Using a plastic spreader, fold the filler over onto itself and into the ribbon of hardener.

17

Using the spreader, scrape the filler and hardener away from the mixing board, and fold it onto itself again.

18

Continue using this folding-over motion from each side until the filler and hardener are thoroughly mixed. The two are thoroughly mixed when the two are one consistent color and there are no streaks.

(continued)

19

Using a clean spreader (use the largest size that will fit into the area being filled), spread the filler onto the surface to be filled. No filler should be more than ⅛ inch thick.

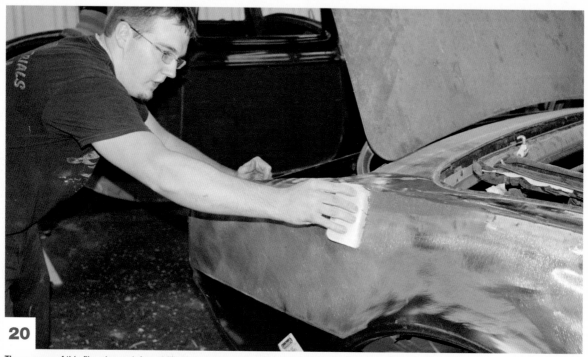

20

The purpose of this fiberglass-reinforced filler is to encase the weld and protect it from the elements that might cause rust to develop later. Apply the filler directly over the weld and to each side, about 2 to 3 inches.

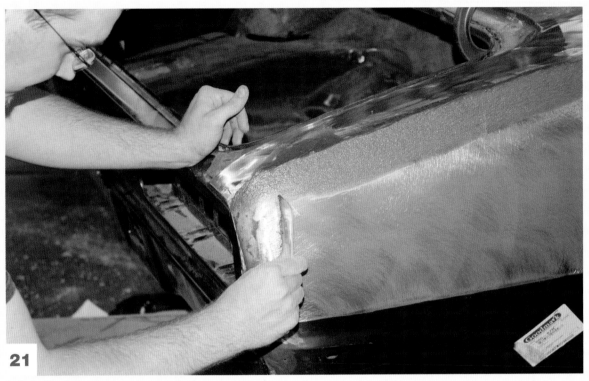

21

Apply the filler to the seam in the more confined areas as well.

22

Much of this filler will be sanded off, but taking a little more time to apply it correctly will require less time to sand it smooth later.

(continued)

RUST REPAIR

23 Again, make sure that the entire welded area is covered to provide the best protection against formation of rust at the weld.

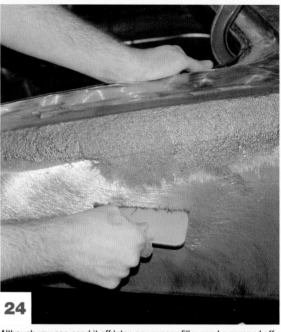

24 Although you can sand it off later, any excess filler can be scraped off with less effort before it begins to set.

25 In this photo, you can see that fiberglass-reinforced filler has been applied along the entire weld and extends down onto the quarter panel about 3 inches. This 3-inch overlap provides room to feather out the filler by sanding it smooth with the adjacent areas.

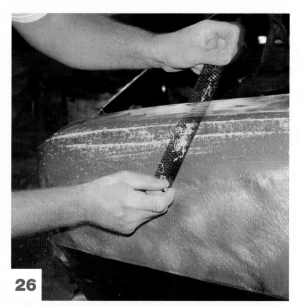

26

You can use 80- or 100-grit sandpaper to smooth the fiberglass-reinforced filler, but a cheese-grater file works better and faster. Some of these files are flat, while others have a rounded shape. The rounded ones seem to be more durable and less likely to break.

27

The filler requires a few minutes to set, but you should begin sanding or filing before it sets completely. When the consistency is correct, the filler will come off in strips, just as cheese would come through a cheese grater.

28

When using a cheese-grater type file, you are only concerned with taking the rough edges or high spots off the filler. It is much smoother than what you started with, but there is still a lot of block sanding to be done.

(continued)

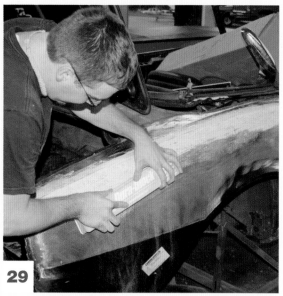

29

With the high spots knocked off, break out your favorite long-board sanding block and some 80- to 100-grit sandpaper. Sand all of the fiberglass-reinforced filler until it is smooth.

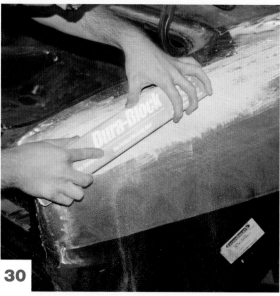

30

By using the longest sanding block that will fit in the area, you will be working toward getting the area flat (not wavy) as well as smooth. More filler will cover this layer, but the sooner you get the filler flat the better.

31

The extra effort to apply the fiberglass-reinforced filler will go a long way toward preventing rust in the weld area where primer was sanded off of the replacement panel.

32

Unless you are a true metal craftsman, you will most likely need to use at least a little bit of filler to get the replacement panel suitable for painting. Starting with no more than 1/8 inch of filler and then sanding most of it off, the filler will end up being merely a skim coat when you are finished. It does, however, provide enough material thickness to sand the body panels perfectly smooth and flat.

RUST REPAIR

33

After mixing the body filler as described previously, the body filler is applied with a spreader. This filler will completely cover the fiberglass-reinforced filler applied previously and will serve to transition between that substrate and the areas that do not have any filler.

34

The filler is first spread onto the panel so that all of the mixed filler is on the area to be filled.

(continued)

Go back with a plastic spreader and smooth out the filler, eliminating ridges in the process. As you mix and use additional filler, you will no doubt learn to use more or less hardener based on how long it takes you to get it spread out and how long you have to wait before you can begin sanding it.

35

If you are going to be working a large area, you will most likely mix the filler and hardener a little cooler so that you will have more time to finesse the filler prior to sanding. However, you do need to mix it stiff enough for it not to fall off of a vertical surface, such as a quarter panel.

36

Although it takes some practice to get the correct amount, try to mix enough filler to cover the entire area within any one panel that you are working on at the time. This will help to eliminate low areas between applications and will allow you to "work" the entire area at one time.

37

RUST REPAIR

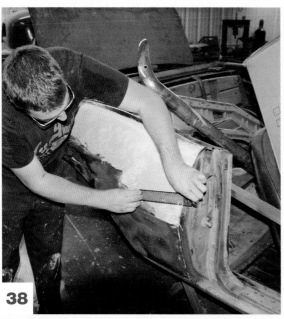

38

When the entire area has begun to set up, you can begin scraping off high spots with a cheese-grater file. If the file causes gouges in the filler, let it sit a while longer. If the filler begins peeling off as it goes through the grater, you are good to go. Working the filler at this consistency will be much easier than when it is fully cured.

39

After you have taken off the high spots with the cheese grater file, flatten and smooth the surface by using a sanding board with 100-grit sandpaper, then with 220-grit, and finally with 400-grit.

40

To eliminate wavy panels, remember to move the sanding board or sanding block back and forth in all directions. However, be careful around bodylines or other ridges so that you do not eliminate the crispness of the sheet metal stamping.

41

Occasionally use an air hose with medium pressure to blow away any buildup of body filler from the sandpaper. Be sure to direct the air pressure away from you and anyone else in the area.

(continued)

RUST REPAIR

HOW TO REPLACE A FULL QUARTER PANEL

Keith Moritz and Brent Schmelz at Morfab Customs were also installing new full quarter panels on an early Chevrolet Nova. The basic procedure is the same as for a partial quarter panel. In this instance, though, the sail panel for the hardtop comes into play.

1 All in all, this Nova is in better condition than others, but there is some rust in the rear quarter panels. The front fenders have already been replaced, and a cowl induction hood installed. The doors are in pretty good shape, so they will be used.

Most of the rust is located around the wheelwell, so a smaller patch panel could be installed. However, if you are paying the going labor rate to have this kind of work done, it is probably not any more expensive to replace the full quarter panel. The dark spot across the sail panel is where the factory-installed lead has been burned away from the seam between the roof and the rear quarter panel.

2

3

At the factory, a fair amount of lead is used to fill and smooth seams where the vehicle designers do not want you to know there is a seam. Before any of these panels can be removed, the lead needs to be burned away with a torch.

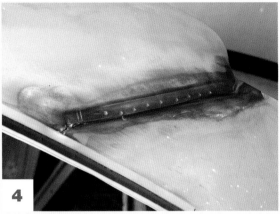

4

This is what the sail panel seam looks like after the lead has been melted away from where the roof and quarter panel meet. With the lead gone, you can see that the roof had a flanged panel that fit to the outside of the quarter panel and was then plug welded.

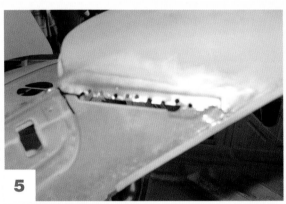

5

On the opposite side of the vehicle, the lead has been melted away and the original quarter panel removed. The replacement panel will need to slide up beneath this overlap.

6

The passenger side quarter panel is slid into position for a test fit. At this point, the quarter sits a little higher than it should. Closer inspection reveals that the lower flange of the replacement quarter is not bent to quite the correct angle.

7

Using a pair of duckbill pliers, Keith carefully folds the lower flange of the replacement quarter panel to the correct shape.

(continued)

A quarter panel never looks as big as it does when it is off the vehicle. Have an assistant help when you are fitting quarter panels. Brent (left) and Keith (right) carefully place the quarter panel into position.

After sliding the quarter panel beneath the roof edge, both check for proper alignment at their respective ends of the replacement panel.

10 Have plenty of clamps handy. Brent already has the quarter panel clamped into place at the top, but is checking to verify that the alignment at the tailpan is correct.

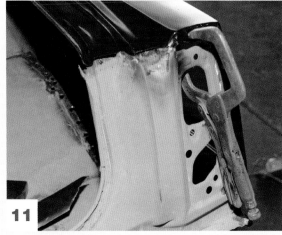

11 The gray area to the left of the clamp is where lead was melted out of the factory seam. You can see that the bodylines that will be exposed when the trunk is opened align quite nicely between the new panel and the old.

12

Initial reaction upon checking the fit is that the quarter panel is a little high at the door, though the quarter is aligned properly. Closer inspection shows an uneven gap at the bottom of the door. By making a slight adjustment at the door hinges, the door will be raised at the back to align with the quarter panel and equalize the gap at the bottom of the door.

13

While Brent is removing the front fender to gain access to the door hinge, the quarter panel looks pretty good overall. Minor adjustments are yet to be made, but there's no rust in the quarter panels anymore.

(continued)

By removing the front fender, you can gain access to the door hinges. Unless you are planning to remove the door completely, loosen the bolts securing the hinges just enough to move the door as desired. When you get the door into the desired position, make sure that you retighten the bolts.

14

While Keith checks the door alignment, Brent loosens or tightens the mounting bolts.

15

16

With the quarter panel in place and verified to align with the door, Brent installs some temporary self-tapping sheet metal screws. The alignment is really good at this point, but the opposite side quarter panel and a replacement tailpan still need to be installed, so it is too soon to weld anything in place.

17

Clamps will still hold the quarter panel at the back, but a few more temporary screws around the door opening will be installed to maintain the correct positioning. After the other replacement panels are installed, the quarter panel can be tack welded in place and the screws will be removed.

RUST REPAIR

Besides the door, you should verify proper alignment between the quarter panel and the trunk lid. You will need to verify that the trunk lid is centered side-to-side and that it is the same height as both of the quarter panels.

After getting the quarter panel secured in place, simply sit back and give it a look from a distance. How do the bodylines line up? Now is the time to find and fix anything that looks amiss.

(continued)

Another look at an area where special
attention needs to be taken to verify proper
alignment. There are several vertical lines in
this area where the full quarter panel should
align with the original tailpan.

Since the center of the tailpan was solid and
in good condition, the original was left in
place, with just the ends being replaced. The
ends of the original tailpan were cut off and
replaced with the end portions that were cut
from the replacement tailpan.

At the taillight area of the tailpan, the quarter
panel is plug welded into place. These welds
should be ground down before any primer
is applied.

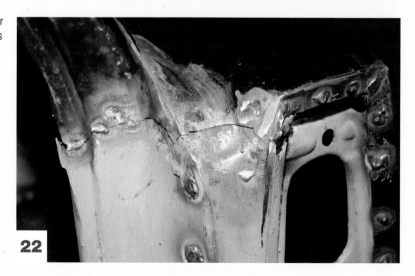

23

The driver side of the tailpan was not in quite as good condition as the passenger side, so more of the replacement panel was used on that side.

24

The driver side replacement quarter panel is installed by following the same procedure as the passenger side. The only difference is the gas filler door, but that is negligible at this point.

(continued)

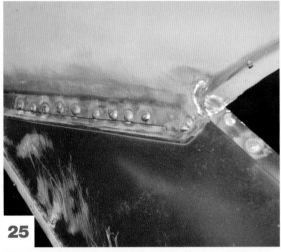

25

After installing the replacement quarter panel, the roof is secured to it with a group of plug welds across the top of the sail panel and down the flange of the rear window opening. These welds are then ground down and the seam between the roof and the quarter panel filled with body filler.

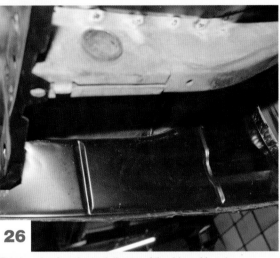

26

This is a shot from beneath the car of the driver side outer wheelhouse and trunk floor dropoff. These pieces fill the gap between the inner wheelhouse and the inside of the quarter panel.

27

Whether doing collision or rust repair, a flourishing automotive aftermarket is making resurrection of many desirable cars a feasible option. So don't be too quick to write off that older vehicle as trash just because it's no longer in pristine condition.

continued from page 120

Rocker Panels

Rocker panels frequently rust out for a variety of reasons. They are located low on the car, therefore requiring a little extra effort to keep them clean when washing the vehicle. Moisture that seeps down the door glass and into the door often drains onto them, but it never dries while the door is closed. Also, rocker panels are often made of folded sheet metal that overlaps the floor panel. This is usually sealed with seam sealer from the factory; when that deteriorates, moisture and debris collect between the panels, causing rust.

Replacement rocker panels are available for most vehicles and are easy to install, requiring only a MIG welder. As with most other replacement panels, you must determine how much of the old panel can be removed. A plasma cutter, die grinder, air saw, tin snips, or whatever tool you have on hand is then used to cut out the old panel. Then tack weld the replacement panel in place to verify correct alignment. You will need to verify that the door will actually open and close without rubbing on the rocker panel. After verifying that the rocker panel is aligned properly, spot weld or stitch weld the rocker panel in place.

Floors

Consisting of two or more sheet metal panels that are flanged to overlap, floor panels are prime targets for rust formation. Although seam sealer from the factory will prevent moisture and dirt from finding their way between these panels for a while, this seam sealer will deteriorate eventually, since it is constantly exposed to the elements. When it does come open, road salt from winter weather, rainwater, along with dirt and debris will work their way between these panels and start forming rust.

Replacement floor panels are becoming more widely available thanks to a growing automotive aftermarket. However, even if replacement panels are not available for your particular vehicle, making new panels is not beyond the abilities of an amateur body man with some basic metal-working skills. Granted, some vehicle floors are considerably simpler than others. Since you will be beginning with flat sheet metal, you should use poster board or other, similar material to make patterns, then transfer the patterns to the sheet metal before cutting the metal. Rather than attempting to cut out one piece of sheet metal and form it to fit the entire area, consider using several pieces, each with simpler bends, and then weld them together as required.

This rocker panel/running board on a 1955 Chevy truck has various damage that will be repaired by installing a replacement panel. Essentially, this piece is folded sheet metal that has some overlap. Seam sealer, even if it was used at the factory, is long gone and rust has begun forming between the panels. Sometimes it is better to replace a panel than to attempt a repair.

The lower portion of this door jamb had some rust-through. With the offending sheet metal cut out, the remaining portion is plug welded to the doorsill.

No commercially manufactured replacement panels are available for this particular area, so a handmade patch was fabricated and then welded in place.

You should also use some method to stiffen the floor so that it does not "oil can" or flex. This can be done by rolling a series of beads into the floor panel with a bead roller or by attaching sheet metal hat channels to the underside. A hat channel is a piece of sheet metal with three sides forming a channel and a brim on the outside, with each side formed by the fourth and fifth sides. This "brim" can then be welded or riveted to the underside of the floor.

continued on page 153

The new floor for this vintage GTO is not finished, but it is well under way. The 18-gauge sheet metal has been cut to the basic size and shape.

Rather than form the floor in one piece with a transmission hump in the middle, floor panels are made for each side. The transmission hump will be formed out of multiple pieces, then welded to the floor panels.

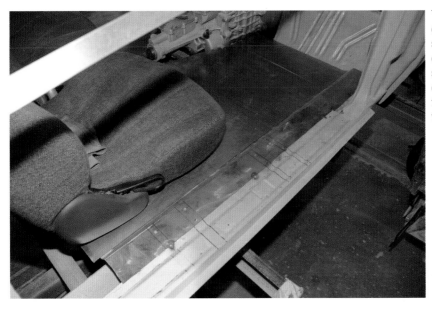

The marks on the doorsill indicate where hat channels will be installed on the underneath side of the new floor panels. Whenever you are constructing a new floor, you need to incorporate some method of stiffening the floorboard. This can be done with hat channels welded on from the bottom or by bead rolling stiffening ribs into the floor panels.

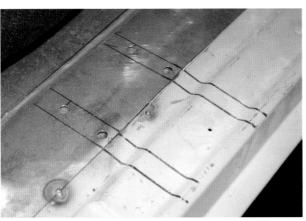

This detail photo shows that the new floor panel is tack welded to the rocker panel. Additionally, lines indicating placement of the hat channels to the underside of the floor panel are extended from the rocker panel to the new floor panel. Holes have already been punched into the floor panel so that the hat channels can be plug welded.

These pieces of sheet metal are hat channels, as their profile resembles a hat. When they are plug welded across the new floor panel, the floor will be reinforced substantially.

Difficult to distinguish in this photo, but this trunk floor is actually made up of three separate panels due to its size. All three are welded to the sheet metal toward the front, which rises above the rear axle and at the back to the tail panel.

HOW TO REPLACE A TAILPAN

The tailpan is the section of sheet metal across the back of the vehicle that connects both of the rear quarter panels, usually also connected to the trunk floor. All of these areas are susceptible to the collection of moisture and dirt, and therefore often require replacement. Keith Moritz and his crew at Morfab Customs were in the process of doing a fair amount of sheet metal work on an early Chevrolet Camaro. They replaced the tailpan in the following way.

The outer tailpan has been removed, leaving the inner tailpan in place. Replacement quarter panels have also been installed. The lower portion of the quarter panels are clamped to the inner tailpan.

After double-checking and verifying proper alignment of the inner tailpan and quarter panels, the quarter panels are plug welded to the inner tailpan.

Brent Schmelz (left) and Keith Moritz hold the outer tailpan in place and look for possible fitment issues. Even though the outer tailpan is light, its span really requires two people to accurately check for proper alignment and fitment.

Although this is a new replacement panel, they are not all perfect. Even if it was perfect when leaving the factory, it is quite possible that some of the thin, flat mounting flanges can get a little out of shape and require a little bit of hammer and dolly work to correct.

Again, the outer tailpan is slid into place and checked for proper fit. You will find that most panels are going to require some minor modifications before they fit correctly. Still, these kinds of fixes are often easier than repairing collision damage, and much more feasible than repairing rust damage.

(continued)

RUST REPAIR

With the panel clamped roughly into position, the passenger side still requires a little bit of persuasion from the back end of a hammer to be positioned correctly.

6

7

Meanwhile, on the driver side, some extra material is being cut off with a die grinder. Quite often, replacement panels will have some extra material. If, for instance, the quarter panels had been incorrectly installed so that they were too far apart at the back. This extra material on the tailpan can come in handy for tying the three pieces together. However, when the quarter panels are installed correctly, the extra material of the tailpan must be removed.

8

Still, some additional material must also be removed from the tailpan. In this case, Brent is using a pneumatic reciprocating saw (that is, an air saw).

9

Back on the passenger side, Keith is using an angle head grinder to remove the paint and primer from the outside of the inner tailpan in preparation for plug welding it to the outer tailpan.

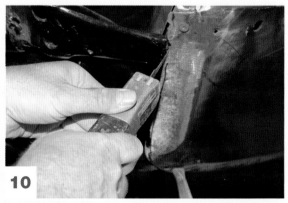

10

Keith uses an air saw to do a little bit of trimming on the passenger side as well.

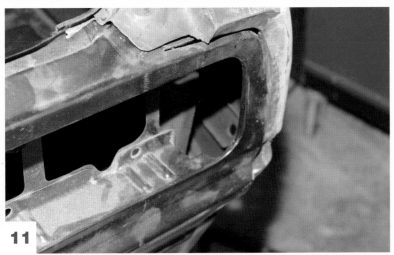

With the excess metal removed, the outer tailpan fits into the opening much better.

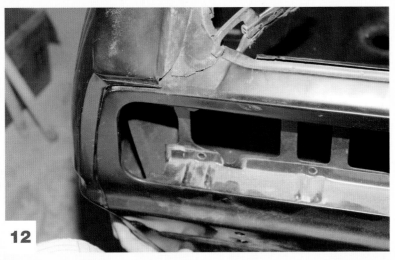

With the tailpan clamped into place, now is the time to verify that everything fits as it should. It is much easier to spend a little bit of time checking now before it is welded in place, rather than later when it would need to be cut out.

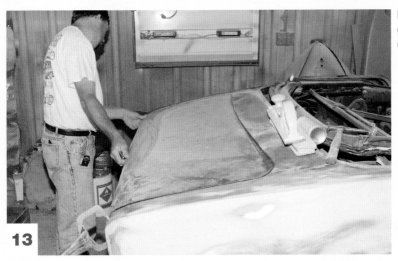

Keith checks the fit of the deck lid and the gaps between it and the newly installed quarter panels.

(continued)

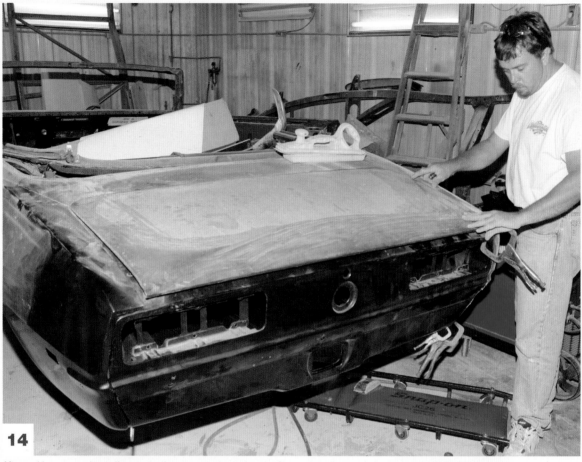

After making some minor adjustments, the gaps are checked again. Check and adjust, and check again, until the fit is correct.

In addition to being stitch welded around the perimeter, the outer tailpan will be plug welded to the inner tailpan in a few places. To help secure the outer tailpan into position with the inner tailpan prior to welding, a bolt is inserted to a common hole in the two and tightened with a washer and nut.

An angle head grinder is then used to remove the primer from the inner and outer tailpan around the perimeter where the two will be stitch welded together.

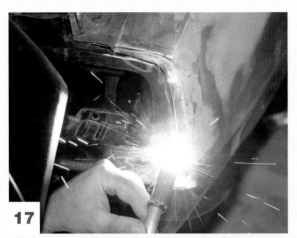

17

Using a MIG welder, Keith then begins the task of welding the outer tailpan in place. Take your time and skip around from one side to the other to minimize any possible heat distortion.

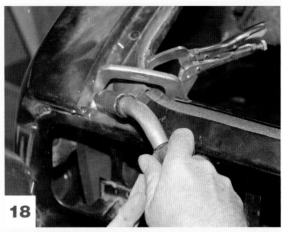

18

Begin the welding process by placing several tack welds around the perimeter so that the panel stays in place, just in case someone inadvertently removes the clamps.

19

At the top of the photo is a series of stitch welds, while a couple of tack welds are visible below. Eventually, stitch welds will go around the entire perimeter.

20

Near the middle of the inner and outer tailpans are some matching holes where the two are to be plug welded together, which Keith is doing here.

(continued)

21

The new tailpan is essentially installed. There is still some more welding to do, but that will take a while to complete.

22

After all of the welding is completed, the various substrates prior to paint application can be applied.

continued from page 144

PANEL REPLACEMENT

Panel replacement differs from patch panel installation, as for this work you are typically installing a complete panel, such as a fender, deck lid, hood, or door skin. This may be a brand-new panel, a reproduction panel, or a used panel from a salvage yard or other parts vehicle. For the most part, panel replacement can be completed with ordinary hand tools, without welding.

Fenders

If you are fortunate enough to have a vehicle well supported by the aftermarket, installing new replacement fenders is pretty simple compared to hammering out a series of dents or removing rust. Front fenders for most vehicles manufactured in the last half of the twentieth century are reasonably priced, making their replacement more feasible than repair if the damage is indeed significant. Of course, minor damage can still be repaired, especially if rust is not a concern.

For the most part, fender replacement is merely a bolt-in operation, though you may need to install shims to obtain the correct alignment with other body panels. Additionally, you will most likely be required to remove some items such as the hood hinge, sidemarker lights, and insignia from the old fender and reinstall them on the new fender.

BODY ALIGNMENT SHIMS

Whether you are reinstalling stock fenders and doors after disassembly for repaint, have repaired collision damage, or are simply replacing parts, the alignment of body panels is important. This is one of those tasks that separates the professionals from the "just get it done" crowd. To get all panels to align perfectly, it might be necessary to install body alignment shims at some of the mounting points. Shims should not be used to make up for shoddy bodywork; still, they may be necessary even if all of the body panels are perfect.

Alignment shims come in a variety of thicknesses and can be stacked as needed to obtain the correct shim thickness. Typically U-shaped, shims can be slid between the two mounting surfaces around a mounting bolt. This allows shims to be installed and removed without completely disassembling the two mounted panels.

Panels should first be installed without any shims and fastened together with the appropriate hardware. If the panels are properly aligned, all is good. If not, you must determine which mounting points require shimming and how much. When that is determined, the appropriate hardware can be loosened slightly,

Since front fender replacement is typically a bolt-on operation, you may want to consider installing a new reproduction fender if rust or collision damage is more than minor. Depending on what climate you are in, beginning stages of rust may be apparent as you begin repairs on your original fender. If you are fighting rust and collision, replacement may be more appealing.

When purchasing body alignment shims, you must know the size of the hardware that they will be used with and purchase shims with the appropriate width slot. Err on the side of too wide rather than too small, or you may end up filing the shim to make it fit. Also purchase multiple thicknesses of shims, if possible, to dial in the fit as accurately as possible.

and a shim of the proper thickness slid in place. The mounting hardware can then be retightened. If a shim of the incorrect thickness was installed, slightly loosen the mounting bolts again and add or remove shims as required.

HOW TO REPLACE A TRUNK FLOOR

Along the lines of "out of sight, out of mind," trunk floors often fall victim to rust-out. All of the junk that we haul in our car trunks bounces around, causing damage over time. Since the trunk floor is typically a combination of several different pieces of sheet metal coming together, the increased damage and trapped dirt eventually lead to rust. However, this is an area where the automotive aftermarket has realized that there is money to be made, so replacement panels are now relatively easy to find for many vehicles that suffer this problem.

To see how to replace the trunk floor in a mid-1960s Mopar, follow along as Morfab Customs' Keith Moritz shows how it is done. The basic steps include cutting out the old sheet metal, replacing the rear subrails as required, then installing the new trunk floor.

1 Trunks come in for a lot of abuse from normal use and exposure to the elements. This means that rusted-out trunk floors are common for many vehicles. The automotive aftermarket realizes this, so replacement panels are currently available for a large variety of automobiles.

The first step toward repair is to verify how much area the replacement panel will cover. Next, cut out the bulk of the rusty sheet metal and get it out of the way. **2**

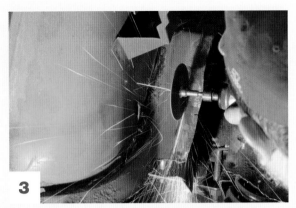

3

With the rusty metal gone, more careful surgery is executed to find out what else must be replaced and how to best attach the new with the old. While a portion of the original subrails were rusty, the forward portion is still solid. Keith carefully trims away some of the remaining trunk floor in order to tie in the new subrail with the old.

4

Continuing with a die grinder equipped with a cutoff wheel, Keith removes additional sheet metal from the top of the inner side of the left side subrail. Prudence is the key here, as you don't want to cut away too much.

5

The new left side subrail is checked for fit. The forward portion will fit into what remains of the original subrail. The rear end of the subrail will attach to the rear body support.

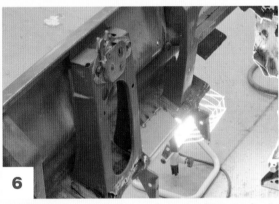

6

Prior to installing the rear body support, some smaller areas of rust were cut out from the tailpan and replaced with flat sheet metal bent to the correct shape. One of these freelance patch panels can be seen located to the left (photo right) of the deck lid latch support.

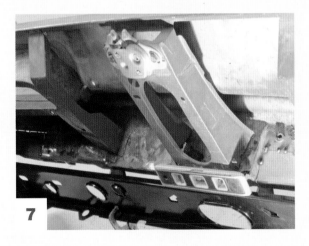

7

With the rear of the body supported by jacks (it is somewhat flimsy since the structural aspect of the floor is now gone) and sitting level, the new rear body support is positioned and checked for level. Clamps are used to secure the rear body support in place for now.

(continued)

While the rear body support is clamped into place, it is also temporarily held with Cleco clamps. These are available in a few different sizes and are used extensively when securing two or more pieces of sheet metal together before they are spot welded together. The sheet metal pieces are aligned, then holes are drilled or punched in both pieces. The Cleco clamps fit through the holes, holding the panel in alignment. The clamps will be removed later and the holes spot welded together.

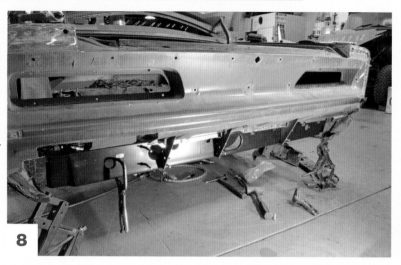

8

These round pins are Cleco clamps. Used not just to hold sheet metal panels together, they also hold them in alignment through the use of common holes in the sheet metal.

9

The left subrail is now set back into place and clamped to the rear body support. Keith looks over the situation to verify that the subrail is positioned as it should be. This includes being located correctly front-to-back, side-to-side, and up-and-down.

10

Some additional trimming is done to the original front subrail to allow the replacement to better fit into position. When making this type of repair, you must also look ahead and determine where the best place will be to make the splice so that you can easily access the location for welding the new to the old.

Another retest fit and Keith is feeling better about the positioning of the new subrail. The front of the subrail is temporarily clamped into position.

The back end of the new subrail is clamped into position.

(continued)

Using a plasma arc cutter, some remaining flange from the wheelwell is cut away.

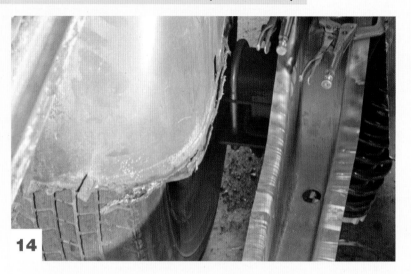

Likewise, a remaining portion of the original trunk floor is cut off.

Even though the front portion of the subrail is clamped into place, Keith is drilling multiple holes in the sides of the original and new subrail so that Cleco clamps can be used to keep them aligned with each other.

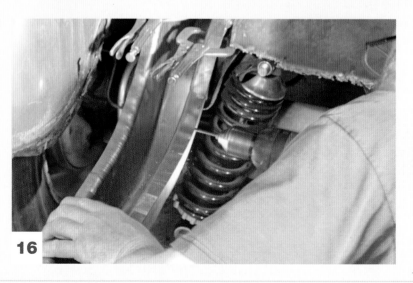

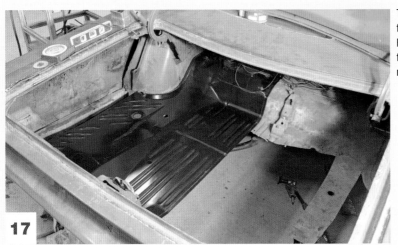

The left side of the two-piece replacement trunk floor is set in place to check for proper fit. For the most part, it looks good. To fit properly, the forward portion of the original floor still needs to be removed.

17

Using a plasma arc cutter, the vertical portion of the original floor was cut loose and removed entirely.

18

19

There is still a portion of original sheet metal atop the rear cross-member held in place with spot welds; this should be removed. After highlighting the location of these spot welds with a wire brush, Keith uses a spot weld cutter to drill them out. At the sound of a slight pop, the sheet metal is free of the spot weld.

20

The left side portion of the original trunk floor has now been completely removed, so the left side of the replacement floor should fit in place properly.

(continued)

21 Prior to tack welding the left side subrail in place, Keith will spray on some weld-through primer on the front end of the new subrail to protect it from rust after being welded in place.

22 After the weld-through primer is applied, Keith uses a sanding disc on an angle head grinder to knock off a couple of burrs on the subrail.

23 The new subrail is then fit into place within the old subrail, clamped into position, and tack welded. The same basic procedure will be followed for the right side. Any necessary adjustments can then be made to provide for a perfect fit.

Keith is using a pneumatic punch to punch holes in the flange of the right side trunk floor. These holes will eventually be the location of spot welds, securing the new right side trunk floor to the new left side trunk floor in approximately the center.

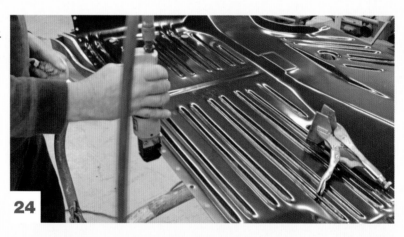

24

Although it is not necessary to remove the quarter panel to replace the trunk floor, having the quarter panel out of the way does give another perspective to the operation. Due to the fact that the wheelhouse requires significant work that lies outside this book's subject, the quarter panel replacement for this particular vehicle will not be shown. However, you can find information on quarter panels elsewhere in this book.

25

RUST REPAIR

26

27

The left side of the new trunk floor has been spot welded to the new subrail, but has not yet been spot welded to the rear body support. After the right subrail and trunk floor have been replaced to this point, the trunk floor panels should overlap by approximately an inch and be spot welded together. Leaving the subrails and trunk floor loose at the rear now allows for any slight adjustment that may be necessary for proper alignment.

Although this is merely a temporary mockup, the new quarter panel will be a vast improvement over the original, which had seen significant rust.

28

With the replacement quarter panel temporarily mocked up, we can see that there is a sizable gap between the trunk floor and the inside of the quarter panel.

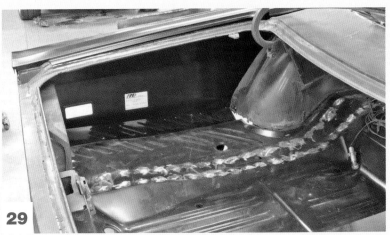

29

The gap will be filled by the new trunk drop after the new quarter panel is installed. This vantage gives us a preview of how the finished product will look.

HOW TO REPLACE A FENDER

Brent Schmelz at Morfab Customs was doing a preliminary fit up on a pair of replacement fenders from the front of an early Camaro convertible. This particular vehicle is undergoing a complete restoration, but some original parts will be used along with replacement parts, making it typical of what you may be faced with during a collision repair job.

1

Front fenders will typically mount to the cowl and the radiator support, along with various other locations. The mounting locations on the cowl will usually be designed so that they can provide vertical and horizontal adjustment through the use of shims.

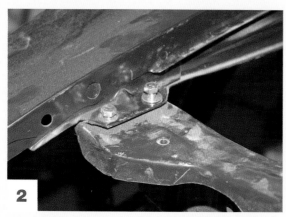

2

The front portion of the fender is secured to the radiator support with two bolts. Some vehicles will have bolts that thread into nuts on the bottom side of the mounting location, while others will require a washer and nut to secure the mounting bolt.

3

After securing the fender to the radiator support, the fender can be pushed or pulled to align the mounting holes at the cowl. You should install all of the mounting bolts loosely, with a couple of turns by hand, before tightening any of them.

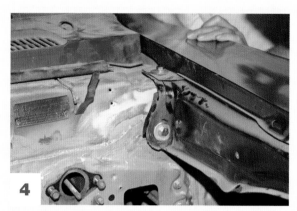

4

The opposite side fender is installed by using the same methods.

5

The hood springs are then secured to the fenders by installing the original hardware in the proper mounting holes in the new fender. Hood hinge mounting locations will vary from make and model, so you may need to refer to the notes you made during disassembly.

6

The hood is then secured to the hood hinge. Do yourself a favor and ask someone for assistance when you install a hood: trying to install a hood by yourself is just asking for more of a challenge than is required.

7

Typically, the hood is secured to the hinge with just two or three bolts on each side. Get them all started by hand and then tighten them all.

8

You can then close the hood to check for proper alignment with the fenders. Be sure to let the hood down gently, but don't force it if it begins to bind. If the hinges are bound up, excessive pressure on the hood can cause it to bend. If the hinges are stiff, apply some lubricant, such as WD-40, to loosen them. If that doesn't work, remove the hood and hinges, clamp the hinge in a vise, apply more lubricant, tap the pivot points with a hammer, and repeat until the hinges work again.

(continued)

RUST REPAIR

9

With the hood operating freely, the nose panel that spans the area between the fenders and in front of the hood should be installed.

10

The hood is secured to the fenders with bolts, washers, and nuts.

The lower fascia that spans the fenders and the underside of the grille is then installed, secured to the fenders with bolts, washers, and nuts.

11

The fit of the fascia should be checked before tightening the mounting bolts completely.

12

13

With all of the front sheet metal components installed, the fit and alignment of the hood can be checked. As seen in this photo, the gap between the hood and the nose panel is greater near the left fender than at the center of the hood. This indicates that the left fender needs to move rearward a bit.

14

Brent loosens the top bolt and then pulls the fender back toward the cowl as required. The mounting bolt is then reinstalled and tightened.

15

Although all of the paint prep work still needs to be completed, we have verified that the front clip sheet metal does fit properly. It may need some tweaking at the final assembly stage, but it is certainly within acceptable limits.

Chapter 8
Surface Preparation & Undercoats

It doesn't matter if you've done bodywork to repair a severely damaged vehicle, simply hammered out a couple of small dents, or are working with brand-new reproduction automotive sheet metal: you need to make the right preparations before you start painting. You will need to apply layers of primers to get the flawless paint finish that your vehicle had when it rolled off the showroom floor.

SURFACE PREPARATION

Even if the repairs you made to collision damage or rust issues was limited to one specific area of your vehicle, you should take the time to make sure the rest of the body is as perfect as can be prior to repainting. A collection of minor parking lot dents in the door is not going to improve the looks of your freshly repaired fender that was repaired simply because it was damaged in a collision. Now is the time to locate all of the little (or not-so-little) dents, dings, and scratches that may have been annoying you for a while. After all, if you've made collision repairs successfully, fixing these minor blemishes should be relatively easy.

Filling Holes

Occasionally, you will have the need to fill small holes in sheet metal. These are usually not the result of collision or rust, but occur when trim has been removed and not used again. As long as the hole is no larger than about a quarter inch in diameter, you can probably simply weld the hole shut. After it is welded closed, grind off any excess that is above the surface and sand it smooth. If the holes are larger than a quarter inch diameter, cut out small pieces of sheet metal, place them over the hole from the backside, and weld them in place. Again, grind off any excess weld and sand it smooth.

The rear fender on the author's '55 Chevy pickup project is in relatively good condition. However, it is not perfect, as it has a relatively minor dent that can be hammered out. There is also a row of holes just above the bodyline. These are small enough to be welded shut, ground smooth, and then covered with a skim coat of body filler.

Filling Low Spots

Many minor door dings can be eliminated without using a body hammer. If the dent is less than ⅛ inch deep, body filler can help eliminate it. Begin by scuffing down the paint in the target area to bare metal or epoxy primer. If you have multiple dents to fill, go ahead and remove the paint from all of the divots. Scoop an appropriate amount of body filler onto a mixing board. Don't mix more than you can apply before it will begin to set up. Apply the appropriate amount of hardener and use a plastic spreader to mix the filler and hardener material thoroughly, until it has consistent color throughout and no streaks. Use a plastic spreader to apply the filler to the dent with a wiping motion in one direction across the dent. If done correctly, the filler will stay in the dent and wipe off the area around it. Use the same method to fill the rest of the dents.

After welding in a new cab corner in the cab of this S-15, a bit of plastic body filler was required to smooth up everything. There is no shame in being required to use some filler to get the area looking correct after making a repair. With the replacement panel properly welded in place and blended in with a bit of filler, no one will ever know any repair was done.

After the filler begins to cure, use some 80- or 100-grit sandpaper on a sanding block to knock off any high spots of filler from around the dent. A gouge in the filler will need additional time to cure. As long as this activity causes dust to appear, continue sanding until the dent is sanded down to the correct level. If necessary, a second coat of filler may be applied to completely fill the area. After rough shaping with 80- or 100-grit sandpaper, sand the entire area with finer sandpaper until blended into the surrounding area.

Sanding

There's no such thing as sanding too much, but if you don't know what you are doing, you can certainly create more problems than you will solve. The main points to keep in mind are (1) use a sanding block or board, (2) use the appropriate grit sandpaper, and (3) sand in an "X" pattern. With these guidelines, sanding is pretty easy. Nevertheless, some hobbyists have been known to get lazy or tired, or try to cut corners, only to minimize the positive effects of the hard work.

Many amateurs waste their sanding efforts simply because they don't use a sanding block or sanding board. They use the palm of their hand instead of spending $10 for a sanding block. For efficient sanding, the sandpaper must make full, even contact with the surface. If you squeeze the palm of your hand in several places, you will find that it is relatively soft in the palm, but harder at the knuckles and joints. Even though your hand can move the sandpaper smoothly across the body surface, more pressure will be applied at the knuckles and less pressure applied at the palm, causing cause waves in the panel due to the uneven pressure placed on the sandpaper as it crosses the body surface.

The appropriate grit sandpaper for the surface to be smoothed depends on whether you are smoothing body filler, color-sanding paint, or something in between. The appropriate grits of sandpaper are discussed elsewhere in this book (Chapter 1). Still, always focus on where you are in the process whenever you pick up a piece of sandpaper.

continued on page 170

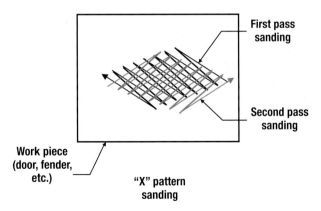

To eliminate the tendency to sand a groove in the panel you are working on, move the sanding board back and forth at approximately 45 degrees from the direction you are moving across the panel. Then, as you work back across the panel, move the sanding board back and forth at approximately 90 degrees to your original sanding pattern.

HOW TO FILL SMALL HOLES

Whether you are carrying out the trim removal process to customize a vehicle or to fill a hole that is no longer needed, filling small holes in sheet metal is relatively easy, if you can weld.

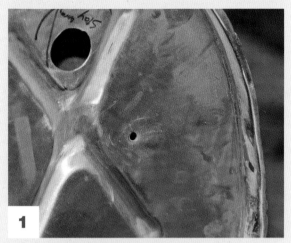

1

While the big hole at the top is necessary, the small hole near the middle of the photo is not required; it will be filled. Many amateur body men would try to fill this hole with body filler and be done with it, but that remedy will most likely fall out sooner or later.

2

This surface is fairly clean. If it wasn't, a grinder or wire brush could be used to clean away any paint, primer, or rust. Some people miss the possibility of rust occurring at the very edge of the hole. This could potentially cause problems with the weld, so use the next-size-larger drill bit to clean the existing hole. This gets rid of any rust or other residue.

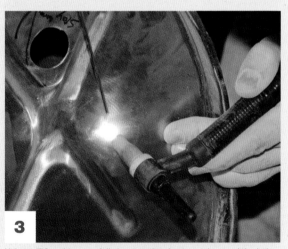

3

Using a TIG welder, carefully heat up the sheet metal around the hole.

4

Insert the filler rod at just the right time.

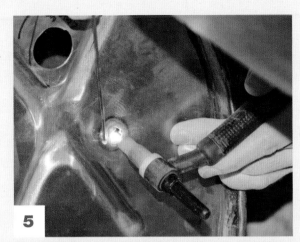

5 By applying heat as required, keep the welding puddle fluid as filler metal is added to completely fill the hole.

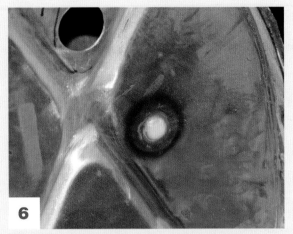

6 Still glowing red hot, we can see that the hole is now filled.

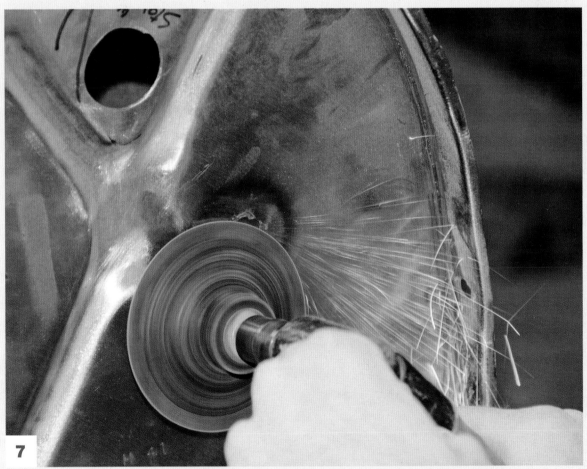

7 Now use a 50- or 80-grit sanding disc on an angle head grinder to smooth the excess weld. Depending on how careful you are with the grinder, this repair may not need any filler, but there is no shame in using a skim coat of filler to feather repairs like this.

continued from page 167

Another amateur mistake is to sand in a simple back-and-forth motion, in the process causing a flat spot or gouge. The correct method is to sand in an "X" pattern by pushing the sander sideways as you make several diagonal passes over the surface, then push the sander back across the area with the sander turned approximately 90 degrees from the first pass. This helps ensure that the entire area is leveled and smoothed evenly.

Getting it Flat and Smooth

When doing bodywork, your objective is to get the repaired panels as straight and flat as possible. That doesn't mean you're trying to remove original bodylines: you are simply (at least in theory) trying to make the surface as smooth and blemish-free as possible. We have all seen natural lakes or manmade reflecting pools that mirror the image of their surroundings. Being liquid, water in these lakes or pools is "flat," allowing it to reflect so perfectly. If you toss a rock or coin in the water and disrupt the flat surface, the reflected image is distorted, even if for a moment. Flat body surfaces on your vehicle will yield the most brilliant paint and allow for the brightest shine. Any imperfections you can find now will be greatly magnified after applying a new coat of paint.

To obtain this flat surface, operate sanding boards and blocks in all directions. Don't simply maneuver them in a back-and-forth direction from front to back: move them up and down and crossways diagonally, rotating the board or block as necessary for ease of operation. This multidirectional sanding technique will guarantee that all areas are sanded smooth without grooves or perceivable patterns.

When satisfied that your filler repair has been sanded to perfection with 240-grit sandpaper, use 320-grit paper to gradually develop a well-defined visual perimeter around the entire repair area. This ring around the repair should expose about an inch-wide band of bare metal and then successive bands of equally wide, exposed rings of primer, sealer,

By sanding in as many different directions as you can, you eliminate waves and actually get the panel flat. Even though this mid-1950s Chevy has lots of contours, the reflections in the paint indicate that the panels are flat like the water of a reflecting pool or mirror.

If you look closely at this photo, you can see that it is the right front fender of a hot rod; this is indicated by the edge of the fender and the tire at the lower left and a portion of the headlight at the upper right. While the guy in shorts is duplicated by the actual contour of the fender, the reflection of everything else (including yours truly) is distortion free. Hours of block sanding were required to obtain this high quality of work.

primer-surfacer, and paint. Because undercoat and paint products consist of different colored materials, you will be able to see your progress clearly. The object, in essence, is to develop a sort of layered valley of smooth walls between the top surface of the body filler area and the top surface of existing good paint. This allows fresh application of undercoat material to fill to the same thickness as those materials already covering the rest of the car's surface.

This "feathering in" process is an important step toward successfully completing any touchup repaint work. Subsequent coats of primer-surfacer material will also be sanded to a point where the only depth difference between an existing painted surface and a repair area will be the actual thickness of the existing paint. Sanding up to this point should find any body filler shaped to the correct contour that will match the panels around it.

Masking

Masking tape will not stick to dirty, greasy, or wax-covered surfaces. Although there might be some initial adhesion, air pressure used when applying primer or paint will cause the masking tape to peel off. Before you begin masking, make sure you spend plenty of time washing those areas where tape will be placed.

Prior to spraying any primer-surfacer to the repaired areas, anything that doesn't receive primer will need to be masked off. Although newspaper has been the traditional materials used to mask, you should avoid it. Newsprint doesn't hold up well to the solvents in paint and primer materials, making its use a risky proposition. Masking paper is available wherever you purchase your primer and paint products and is relatively inexpensive when compared to its ease of use and effectiveness.

Use masking paper and automotive grade masking tape to mask the areas that are in the direct path of the application of primer or paint. To cover larger areas that are not in the direct path of primer or paint, find large plastic masking material at automotive paint retailers. Similar to food-wrapping material, this plastic is very thin. In contrast, the plastic sheeting you might use as a paint drop cloth when painting the inside of your house is much too thick and heavy for use on automobiles.

An initial estimate of the masking needs for your vehicle may appear to be rather limited and easy to accomplish. However, understand that less-than-meticulous masking will almost always result in obvious spots of overspray, imperfections that clearly indicate sloppy work or are regarded as signs of inexperience. Some paint overspray can be cleaned off, but proactive masking is much easier than reactive cleaning.

Next to color matching, masking is perhaps the most meticulous and exacting chore required of an auto body painter. Since your auto body paint and supply store will mix paint blends and tints, your most precise work revolves around masking. To make the job as simple as possible, devise and follow a systematic masking plan, then allot enough time to complete those tasks with strict attention to detail.

Painting panels that are located near windows always present more of a problem when masking, as there are usually several pieces of molding and trim surrounding the glass. Of course, the most efficient way to avoid the errant application of paint is to remove the trim, molding, and glass; this isn't always a practical solution, though. If these areas must be masked, do yourself a favor and purchase a roll or two of ⅛-inch Fine Line masking tape, in addition to the automotive grade masking tape and masking paper that you need for the job.

Whether the work is done in a commercial spray booth or your home garage, proper masking is a must when priming and painting. For masking small areas (door openings, glass, or portions of a panel that is being painted), masking paper secured with masking tape provides the best results. For areas that are not going to be in the direct line of spray, but still need to be protected from overspray, masking film is the best bet. It is thin and lightweight, but can be spread over a large area quite easily.

Outline the area to be masked with your ⅛-inch Fine Line tape, making sure that it covers the very edge of whatever is being masked, then attach ¾-inch automotive grade masking tape to the Fine Line tape. For narrow areas, such as window trim, one or two additional strips of tape will probably cover the area to be masked. If you are masking a large area, secure masking paper to the first piece of ¾-inch masking tape. Be sure to use masking tape to cover any seams in masking paper.

When masking window glass, only one piece will be needed, as long as the masking paper is wide enough to reach from the top to the bottom of the window. Fold the paper as necessary so that it fits neatly along the sides of the glass. Use strips of masking tape to hold the masking paper in place. If the glass you are masking is wider than the masking paper, use two or three strips of masking paper placed horizontally to cover all of the glass. Lightly secured paper edges will blow open during spray paint operations and allow mists of overspray to infiltrate spaces beneath paper. For this reason, always run lines of tape along the length of paper edges to seal off underlying areas completely. This is especially important when the edge of one piece of masking paper is lapped over another.

Masking paper doesn't always come in widths that fit window shapes exactly. Most of the time, especially with side windows, you end up with a tight fit along edges and bulges in the middle. To avoid bulges, fold excess masking paper so that it lies flat. Not only does this make for a tidy masking job, it prevents bulky paper from being blown around by air pressure from a paint spray gun. All you have to do is lay one hand down on an edge of the paper and slide it toward the middle. With your other hand, grasp the bulging paper and fold it over. Use strips of tape to hold it in a neat fold.

If the windshield and/or back window in your vehicle is secured by large, flexible rubber molding, masking it can be made easier by sliding a length of soft, non-scratching cord under it. This will elevate the rubber molding away from the surface to be painted and allow you to apply masking tape to the edge underneath and wrap it around the top of the molding.

Although most painting jobs call for the removal of emblems and badges, there are two occasions when they can be left in place. This is when clear coat paint is the only material scheduled to be sprayed over them, and when spot painting work will require only a light melting coat be applied close to their edge. In either case, careful masking must be done to ensure that no overspray is allowed to build up on their face or edges. Intricate masking with tape is needed to ensure emblem and badge edges are completely covered, while no part of the tape extends onto the painted surface. Take your time placing tape over item edges first, before being concerned with masking surfaces. Again, Fine Line tape may be the best material for this meticulous task. After attaching the tape's end to a corner of an emblem, maneuver the roll with one hand while carefully placing and securing the tape with your other hand. Practice is essential, so don't expect to accomplish this kind of unique masking on the first try.

Some painters make the job easier by covering emblems with wide strips of tape first. Then use a sharp razorblade to cut the tape along the emblem edges at the exact point where they meet the painted body. Use a very delicate touch to avoid cutting into paint or missing the mark and leaving an open gap along the part being masked off. If you decide to try this technique, make very light passes with the razorblade, even if it takes two or three attempts to cut completely through the tape. This will prevent excessive pressure on the razorblade from cutting deeply into the sheet metal.

Since door locks and handles mount directly to door panels, the same kind of meticulous masking is required for them as for emblems and badges. If possible, remove door locks and handles to ensure uniform coverage of primer and paint on the door surface. If it is not feasible to remove these pieces, use ¾-inch tape to mask the perimeter edges, then 2-inch tape to completely cover the unit. Remember, the most critical part of masking is along the edge, where items meet painted panels. Wide strips of tape can easily cover faces and other easy-to-reach parts.

Key locks are the easiest to mask by simply covering them with a length of 1- or 2-inch wide tape. Use your fingernail to force tape down along the circumference, to be sure coverage is complete and that the tape is securely in place. Then cut the excess from around the lock's circumference with a sharp razorblade.

Do not forget to mask doorjambs before spraying primer and paint. You would be surprised how much unwanted paint can find its way between a closed door and the doorjamb. If your bodywork plan calls for the priming and painting of door edges and doorjambs, these edges should be painted first and allowed to dry. After they have cured sufficiently for masking tape and paper to be applied, the inside portion of the door and the doorjamb can be masked off. The door can then be closed and the exterior primed and painted.

Use the same procedure if you are replacing the doors. It is much easier to paint the interior side and perimeter edges of doors while they are off the vehicle. The doors can then be installed on the vehicle, the door edges and doorjambs masked off, and then the exterior panel painted along with the rest of the body.

Some painters like to apply 2-inch tape along the edges of rear doorjambs with the sticky side facing out. With this technique, only about half of the tape strip actually goes on the jamb; the rest is folded over so that it is perpendicular. Another strip is placed on the rear door edge in the same manner: half of it sticks out, with the sticky side facing out. This way, when the door is closed, both strips of tape are attached to each other to effectively seal the gap between the door and jamb.

The same technique is used along the lower door edge. For front doors, tape is applied to the front edge of the rear door to match the rear edge of the front door when it is closed. Perfecting these maneuvers calls for a little practice and some patience. Tape doesn't always stick the way you would like and, sometimes, the air movement caused by a door closing is enough to throw off the tape's ability to match up with a corresponding strip.

Two-inch tape and 4- to 6-inch paper can be used to mask doorjambs and edges. However, consider where the tape edges are placed: if they're set too far out, they may allow a paint line to be visible through the gap between the door and the jamb. This is an important factor when painting a color on the exterior that contrasts with the shade on the doorjambs. You have to decide where the dividing line will be and make sure you position the tape symmetrically.

When masking drip rail molding, pay close attention to the top inner side as well as the facing portion. Place an adequate width of tape to mask the inner side first, then lay it down over the face. Should another strip be needed, apply it to the bottom edge first and fold excess over the front to overlap the previous strip.

Masking other types of trim doesn't require any special skill, other than patience and attention to detail. Edges next to body panels should be covered first and the face covered last. Hold a roll of tape in one hand and position the extended strip with the other directly on top of trim sections. Be absolutely certain that trim edges are covered and that tape doesn't extend onto the body. Small pieces of tape that touch body parts will block paint from the surface to cause a blemish.

Rather than wrap a radio antenna with masking tape in a "barber-pole" fashion, sandwich the antenna with two strips of masking tape pressed together along each edge, then secure these two pieces with additional tape to cover the antenna's base.

Taillights and side-marker lights are usually easier to remove than to mask. Simply remove the mounting screws, unplug the light bulb, and set the taillight assembly aside. Make sure that you mask the wires and the bulb so that your work doesn't look like an amateur did it. However, should you decide to mask taillights instead of removing them, plan to use strips of 2-inch tape. Because their designs commonly feature curved corners or awkward shapes, masking is accomplished much easier, faster, and more completely by placing overlapping strips of 2-inch tape over their entire surface. Be sure that each overlap extends to at least ¾ inch over; this will prevent paint seepage into seams. Side-marker lights are masked off using the same procedure as for emblems and badges.

If you need to prime or paint the area directly behind a bumper, this piece should be removed to allow complete access, rather than masking the bumper and spraying around it. If you are simply protecting the bumper from overspray, fold masking paper over the top edge of the bumper and tape it in place. Wrap the paper over the face of the bumper and fold the paper as necessary so that it wraps around the lower edge, then tape the bottom edge and the seams.

To mask the front grille of your vehicle, open the hood and tape a piece of masking paper across the top of the grille so that the paper hangs down in front. Trim or fold the paper as necessary, then tape the edges of the paper along the edge of the grille. If additional pieces of masking paper are necessary, be sure to cover the seams with masking tape.

On vehicles with painted fender wells, take time to adequately cover them with masking paper and tape. You don't need to mask normal, everyday-driver fender wells covered with undercoat, unless you have a specific desire to do so. On these, cover overspray imperfections with new layers of undercoat or black paint.

Plastic covers for wheels and tires are available for use to mask them from overspray, but some large plastic trash bags will also work. Just be sure to secure the bags so that they don't come off during your spraying session. If you do inadvertently get some paint on your tires, scrub them clean with the same paint reducer that you are using with your paint.

At around $75, a masking paper dispenser may not be a justifiable expense for a one-time repair, but if you do much masking for priming or painting, it can save you a lot of time. This dispenser applies masking tape to one edge of the paper as it is dispensed, making the paper easier to secure as you put it in place. More expensive models contain various widths of paper.

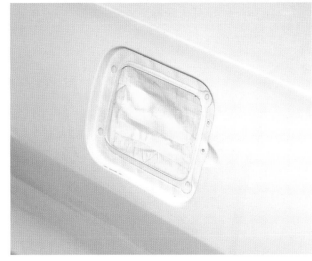

This masking of a gas filler opening may not be very impressive to most. However, taking a little extra time to mask this properly will prevent you from having new paint and primer on the gas cap and the filler neck. Not a big deal, but it is something that will separate those who seek professional results from the amateurs who don't care.

Always inspect your masking work after the tape has been positioned. Use a fingernail to guarantee that the tape is securely attached along the edges. You may have to lie down in order to accurately place masking tape on the undersides of body side trim. Do whatever it takes to accomplish your goal of masking so that nobody will notice that any paintwork was done—except that the car body looks great.

UNDERCOATS

Just because the dents have been hammered out and a coat of body filler applied doesn't mean that you're ready to spray paint. Oh, you could, but if you were to apply paint at this point, the finished vehicle would look like a spotted mess. You wouldn't get the undamaged, smooth finish your vehicle had before the accident. If you have performed all of the necessary bodywork and done it correctly, now is certainly not the time to lose sight of finishing the task with the same care and attention to detail. Even if you can't justify painting the affected area for whatever reason (matching body panels don't matter to you, you don't have a place to apply paint, or you simply can't afford the paint), at least apply a uniform coat of primer to the repaired area.

Don't confuse undercoats with the sticky black tar substance that's applied to the underneath of new vehicles to minimize rust through. For the purposes of auto body repair, undercoats are the necessary substrates of various primers that precede the application of paint and other top coats. Paint and these other top coats are discussed in detail in Chapter 9. Undercoats provide basic corrosion protection to bare metals, increase adhesion of whatever substrates or top coats that follow, and provide a surface that can be sanded smooth. Since undercoats in general perform a multitude of tasks, specific types of primers must be used for each step of the priming process.

Cleaning

After sanding or scuffing has been successfully accomplished, perform a thorough cleaning to remove all surface contaminants. Painters normally use air pressure to blow off layers of sanding dust from body surfaces, as well as between trunk edge gaps, door edges, and doorjambs.

With the bulk of dry dust and dirt removed by air pressure, painters use wax and grease remover products to thoroughly wipe down and clean body surfaces. Each paint manufacturer has its own brand of wax and grease remover that constitutes part of an overall paint system.

continued on page 180

175

Whether you are going to repair and repaint your damaged vehicle or just make it drivable and spray on some primer, you need to mask off the areas where you don't want primer and paint. You may simply be masking off the glass before repainting the entire body, or limiting the new paintwork to just a localized area, such as two doors and a fender. Follow along as one of the body men from Jerry's Auto Body masks a four-door sedan prior to applying primer-surfacer.

Prior to masking the outside of the vehicle, it is wiped down with wax and grease remover. Just as paint will not stick to dirt and other contaminants, neither will masking tape. You certainly don't want the masking tape and paper to start coming loose when you are in the middle of spraying primer-surfacer or, even worse, while spraying the final paint.

1

2

Prior to masking, take a moment to determine what actually needs to be masked and what needs to be left open. Areas that must be left open include the section from about the middle of the front door to the edge of the body, where it meets the rear bumper/fascia, and from the bottoms of the windows to the bottom edge. First a piece of wide masking paper is used to cover the front half of the front door. For primer-surfacer application, this wide piece of masking paper will provide sufficient coverage for the front portion of the car. Additional masking will be necessary when the topcoat of paint is applied.

3

A piece of tape is attached to the bottom edge of the car from the inside so that a piece of masking paper can later be attached to it. This will act as a skirt to prevent overspray from being on any of the underneath side of the vehicle.

4

The front door is now opened and tape placed along the inner edge of the door. Masking paper will be taped to this first piece of tape and then folded to the inside of the door. This protects the doorjamb and doorpost from overspray through the gap between the doors.

The same procedure of masking the doorjamb will be repeated on the back door as well. Performing this step carefully will ultimately save more time, as you will not need to come back and sand off overspray from the doorjambs.

5

(continued)

Although it is a relatively small opening, it is still necessary to close up the space vacated by the removal of the outside door handle, as much primer-surfacer would find its way into the car. This opening is not being masked off from paint application, as all of the outside should be coated with primer-surfacer and then paint. For this reason, it has to be masked from the inside, instead of the outside, as with work done on windows. With the door open and the interior door panel removed, two pieces of wide masking tape can be overlapped to close off this opening.

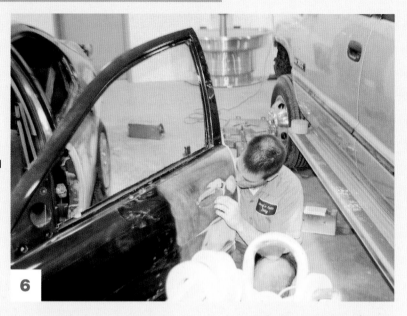

6

7

Even though there may seem to be no reason for removing the interior door panels, tasks like closing the opening vacated by the removal of the door handle make it a necessity. Some people might just leave the interior door panel in place and use it to prevent paint from getting inside the car. That, however, would be a very unprofessional way of doing the work.

8

With the interior door panel removed, we get a glimpse of the inside of the door. Shown are the window riser mechanism (don't pinch your fingers), the connecting rod to the door latch, and wiring for power door locks.

9

With a skirt along the bottom of the vehicle, masking paper is now used to mask off the windows. Primer-surfacer will not be applied above the bottom edge of the windows or above that imaginary line, as it would cross the rear quarter panel. Therefore, the masking paper is aligned with the lower edge of the window only and simply draped over the window, instead of masking only the glass area.

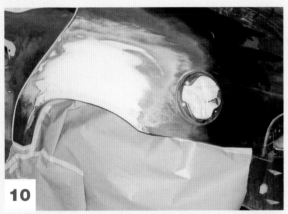

10

Much like the opening in the door for the door handle, the gas filler door must be masked from behind as well. Masking tape is now applied to the inner edge of the wheel well to serve as an attachment point for masking paper to cover the wheel and tire. The paper is folded over as necessary to completely cover the wheel and tire, yet still be out of the way so that the wheel well is accessible for paint application.

11

This Dodge sedan is almost masked sufficiently for the application of primer-surfacer. Note that the primer-surfacer will extend beyond the actual repair area, yet not completely to the masked edge. When the actual painting is done, the entire left rear quarter panel along with both doors will be painted. To fully match the rest of the car, it may be necessary to blend clear onto the trunk, the roof, and the front fender.

continued from page 174

Only use the wax and grease remover products that are deemed part of the paint system you will be using; this will ensure that it is compatible with the rest of your painting materials.

Dampen a clean cloth (heavy-duty paper shop towels work great) with wax and grease remover and use it to thoroughly wipe off all body surfaces in the area of expected paint undercoat applications. The mild solvents in wax and grease removers loosen and dislodge particles of silicone dressings, oil, wax, polish, and other materials embedded in or otherwise lightly adhered to surfaces. To assist the cleaning ability of wax and grease removers, follow the damp cleaning cloth with a clean, dry cloth in your other hand. The dry one picks up lingering residue and moisture to leave behind a clean, dry surface. Use a new towel on every panel, wipe wet, then dry the surface *thoroughly*.

Primer-Surfacer

An application of primer-surfacer will quickly provide you with visual evidence of how complete your bodywork is. What may look great when still in bare metal or body filler will show every low or high spot or other blemish. Although primer-surfacer is often described as "high-build primer," it should not be used as body filler. If there are indeed low spots that should be filled, use additional body filler to accomplish this.

Begin by cleaning the area with wax and grease remover, then use a tack rag to remove dust particles and lint. Be sure to mix the primer-surfacer and reducer per the mixing instructions on the label, then apply two or three coats of primer-surfacer to all areas where bodywork has been done. Make sure that you allow the proper flash time between coats. If you have several localized spots of repair on one panel, or adjacent panels, go ahead and apply primer-surfacer to the entire panel rather than just to the spots where repair work has been done. This will give you a better chance to blend the surfaces during the block sanding process.

After the primer-surfacer has had ample time to cure, spray a light but uniform mist coat of SEM's Guide Coat (or any contrasting color spray-can enamel) onto the areas to be sanded. After this guide coat dries, break out your favorite sanding board with some 320-grit sandpaper and block sand the entire area where primer-surfacer has been applied. The guide coat will quickly disappear from high spots, but not from low spots.

After this initial sanding with 320-grit, it should be obvious if any additional filler is required. If this is the case, add it as needed, shaping it with 100- and 240-grit sandpaper, then apply two or three coats of primer-surfacer to all areas where you have placed the additional filler. Block sand these areas again with 320-grit sandpaper. If the body is at the proper contour after sanding with 320-grit sandpaper, switch to 500-grit sandpaper and block sand the entire area again.

Sanding with finer sandpaper grits will focus on texture smoothness as well as the removal of sanding scratches and very shallow imperfections. Using the longest sanding board or block available with progressively finer sandpaper is the key to achieving the straightest and flattest surface upon which to apply paint.

Sealer

Sealer is typically the last of the undercoats to be applied before color. Before starting, complete all bodywork and sanding and mark off any areas that are not to receive sealer. The purpose of the sealer is, as the name suggests, to seal in all of the various undercoats and fillers and keep them from seeping into the top coats. The sealer will also provide a base to allow for uniform color coverage and aid in adhesion of the top coats.

Before applying sealer, use an air hose to blow dust and dirt out of all cracks and crevices. Clean the surface with wax and grease remover, and confirm that you have masked off all areas that shouldn't receive sealer. Blow off the surface again using an air hose, clean again with wax and grease remover, and go over the area with a tack cloth. Mix the sealer by following the directions, set the air pressure as directed, and put on your protective gear, if you haven't already. Spray sealer first over the areas where filler has been applied, then feather the sealer toward the masked edges, but do not spray all the way to the edge. Allow the sealer to flash dry per the directions, then apply second and third coats with the appropriate time between coats.

Don't sand sealer unless runs or other imperfections occur. If that happens, allow the sealer to dry, use fine-grit sandpaper to remove the blemish, and then touch up with more sealer. Once the sealer has cured according to the label directions, paint can then be applied.

Seam Sealer

Many adjacent panels are simply plug welded together at the factory, which is one of the reasons that vehicles start accumulating rust. Even though seam sealer is applied between the welds to seal these seams during manufacture and hold the panel together sufficiently,

For a guide coat, most any contrasting color of spray-can enamel can be used. It should be sprayed on lightly, but uniformly.

If the guide coat is indeed sprayed on uniformly, the panel should be flat (without ripples) when all of the guide coat is sanded off.

This early Camaro body has already received the bodywork that was required. However, before spraying any paint, a guide coat has been applied. With a uniform covering of contrasting paint color (spray cans work great for this), light block sanding will quickly reveal any high or low spots that may have been missed previously.

HOW TO SPRAY PRIMER-SURFACER

Spraying primer-surfacer is easy to do, but you have to make sure it's done correctly: the rest of the paint process is based on this step. At this point, you still have plenty of sanding to do, so don't be concerned with runs and sags, as they can be sanded out during the block sanding process. This may be the first time you have ever used a spray gun. At minimum, you will need to adjust the gun to the recommended air pressure setting for the material you are spraying. Do some practice spraying on something before turning to your vehicle's body parts. Follow along as a sedan is prepped for paint at Jerry's Auto Body.

After all of the masking is completed, but before any primer-surfacer is applied, the area to be primed is cleaned again with wax and grease remover. Although you can apply the wax and grease remover with a clean paper towel and wipe it off with another, most professionals apply it with a spray bottle and then wipe off the wax and grease with a clean paper towel.

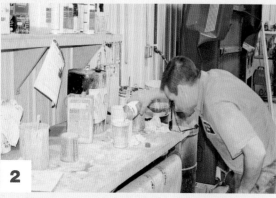

Even primer-surfacer should be carefully mixed to ensure its proper application. Using a calibrated mixing cup makes mixing primer-surfacer with reducer quite easy. Be sure to read the mixing instructions to verify the correct ratio. After thorough mixing by stirring, a paint strainer is placed in the spray paint cup, followed by the primer-surfacer. Never pour any kind of paint product into a spray paint cup without a strainer. There's no excuse not to have one, as strainers are usually available for free where you purchase your paint. If you don't use a strainer, you risk ruining your expensive spray gun if a speck of dirt or debris gets into an orifice that can't be cleaned.

Primer-surfacer shouldn't be sprayed all the way to the masking paper, because this will create a harsh line at that point. Instead, the primer-surfacer should taper from a heavier application at the actual repair to a very thin dusting before reaching the mask line.

the seam sealer eventually falls out, allowing moisture and dirt to find their way between the panels. Over time, this will cause rust and corrosion at the mating surfaces and, the next thing you know, the panels are falling apart. The seam sealer from the 1960s and 1970s was not as high quality as it is today.

When making repairs, there are two methods for preventing rust from reoccurring in these rust-prone areas. The best way is to minimize the opportunity by stitch welding all of the panels together. This greatly minimizes the potential for rust, as there are no open seams to attract and accumulate dirt, debris, and moisture. If you are not actually replacing panels, or complete welding is not feasible, you can apply new seam sealer.

If the components to be sealed are going to be stripped (mechanically or chemically), do this first, then apply epoxy primer. Any existing seam sealer should be removed before installing new seam sealer. To apply seam sealer, you need to clean all metal surfaces, but you don't have to remove primer or paint. Seam sealer is available either in a dispensing tube that works with a caulking gun or in a tube that can be squeezed by hand. In either case, simply apply a bead along the seam between the two adjacent panels.

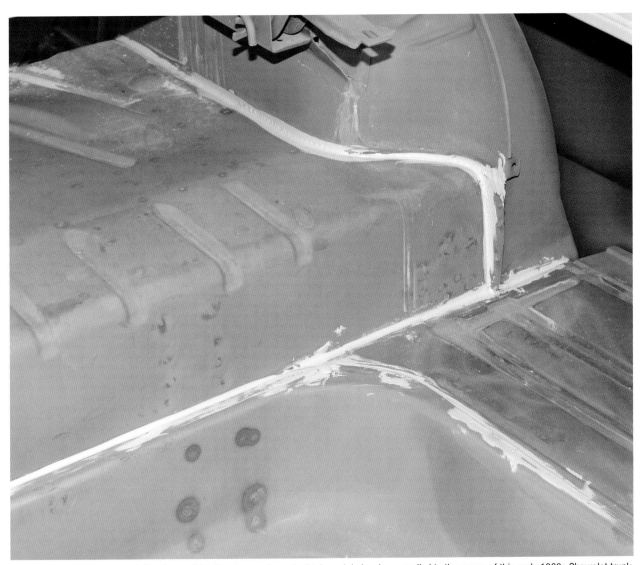

Seam sealer, which looks much like the caulking found around your bathtub or sink, has been applied to the seams of this early 1960s Chevrolet trunk. Since this large area consists of several smaller pieces of sheet metal that are welded together, there is more than ample opportunity for moisture, dirt, and debris to find their way between the overlap of these panels. The seam sealer keeps this from happening and therefore minimizes the opportunity for the formation of rust.

Chapter 9
Painting: Color & Other Top Coats

Painting an automobile, the actual practice of applying paint to the vehicle's surface, is relatively easy. Mixing some paint pigment, reducer, and hardener together, pouring the concoction into a spray gun cup, and pulling the trigger—although it shouldn't be taken lightly, this process is simple and straightforward. We will cover each of these steps things later. However, regardless of what anyone tells you, the body straightening, block sanding, and other surface preparation is generally what makes or breaks a paint job. Sure, you could do something stupid when you apply paint, but short of having brain fade while doing it, painting is really the easiest part of the bodywork process.

Each step you take while performing body repair and surface preparation will have a direct impact on the overall outcome, so each step must be done as precisely and accurately as possible. In other words, every time you set out to accomplish some kind of preparatory or actual paint chore, make sure it is done correctly the first time. If you do run into problems or can't get the results you desire, take the time you need to adequately repair or remove any imperfections to make that phase of the process perfect.

All body-surface preparation jobs focus on a single goal: a perfect paint job. However, each has its own function, and one won't improve or cover another's lack of perfection. With this in mind, take your time during each preparatory phase and don't go on to the next step until you are satisfied that the work you just did has been accomplished accurately and completely.

Auto body surface preparations include jobs that actually get surfaces ready for paint application. Depending on the specific project, these tasks may consist of, but are not limited to, part dismantling, old paint and rust accumulation removal, primer material application, finish sanding, and surface cleaning with wax and grease remover and tack cloths. If these are carried out haphazardly, the next operation cannot possibly be accomplished correctly. We have already discussed these processes, so if you are feeling hesitant about your bodywork or paint prep, go back and reread the relevant sections, then go back and redo anything that you didn't get quite right. Revisiting these steps may seem like a lot of additional work, but it is easier to retrace your steps before you paint, rather than waiting until after the paint is applied, at which point you may wish that you had taken a little extra time in the preparation.

PAINT SCHEME

If you have simply repaired some minor collision damage on your daily driver, you will most likely want to paint the affected panels to match what they looked like before the collision. Whether you want to use one color or a couple depends on your particular vehicle and where the damage occurred. If you were lucky, the damage was limited to just one panel, in an area that was only one color. In reality, though, Murphy's Law as it applies to bodywork dictates that damage will extend to multiple panels and involve every color imaginable. On most production vehicles that have a two-tone paint scheme, the color is usually broken at a bodyline so that masking is more easily accomplished. Additionally, there is usually some sort of trim that covers the edge of the different covers. Determine the extent of the necessary repainting efforts *before* you are actually ready to start spraying paint. All too often, the amateur body man has a hard time conceiving just how large an area is affected when making a repair to what first looked like a small dent.

This doesn't change how you will proceed, but you should realize that anything other than a monotone paint job will require additional work. Except for detailed custom airbrush work, such as that found on hot rods or race cars, each color of paint to be sprayed will require that you mask off the entire vehicle—except, of course, the area you are spraying. If you have masked the vehicle properly one time, you can do it again, though that may be more than what you care to try if this is your first time painting a vehicle.

When applying multiple colors, it is even more critical to observe the proper flash and drying times for the paint system you will use, *before* masking. Applying masking tape or masking paper to freshly painted surfaces that haven't fully dried can make a huge mess of your paint job. Product information sheets for the specific type of paint you are using will provide a recommended time for the paint to dry before taping. Likewise, clear coats (if applicable) must be applied within a specified time, or the base coat will need to be scuffed and additional base coats added.

Monotone

Since the collision damage has been repaired to a like-new condition, matching the paint is your most significant remaining hurdle. Assuming that you are not making a complete color change (more about that in a moment), you will need the color code for your vehicle in order to purchase the correct paint color. Information for this code is usually included on the VIN tag or the color and options tag. These tags are found on the driver's doorjamb, in the glove box door, or somewhere under the hood. If you can't find the tag for your vehicle, check with your automotive paint supplier: they will usually have resources that show where the color code tags are, as long as you can tell them your make and model.

When you take your paint code number to the paint supplier, they can put the number into their paint mixing program and provide the amount of paint you want in the color that matches what was on your vehicle when it rolled out of the factory. However, on occasion, the paint code doesn't match what is actually on the vehicle. Although the percentage of mismatched paint codes is small, there is a chance that this may happen to you, considering with the great number of production vehicles built each year. Additionally, your vehicle may have been completely repainted in its lifetime. After the paint store staff determines your factory color, but before getting a couple of gallons mixed for you, verify that the paint is basically blue, yellow, red, or whatever you expect it to be. If your vehicle is blue, but the paint code turns out to be yellow, something is amiss.

Although there are many opportunities to practice perfect masking, such as around the lights, a monotone vehicle is easier to mask for painting.

Although this mid-1950s Chevrolet relies heavily on trim to break the multicolor layout, it still presents a challenge when masking if all of the trim has been removed. Before doing a multicolor paint job, you should make plenty of notes to be sure that you get it right on both sides.

For a simple monotone paint job, you can clean the vehicle with wax and grease remover, mask off whatever isn't going to be painted, remove any dust with a tack cloth, and then apply the paint. If you plan on changing your vehicle's color completely, even a monotone paint scheme will be a bit more complicated. The majority of the additional work will be under the hood and the interior of the vehicle. The only correct way to paint under the hood requires removing the engine, as you simply don't have enough room for maneuvering, masking properly, and painting the firewall. On older, larger vehicles, you may be able to paint the inner fenders by using a detail spray gun. On the inside of the vehicle, remove everything that you can so that you can avoid masking it. Many vehicles have surfaces painted in a neutral color that can be used as-is, even if the exterior color has changed. Whether the interior color and your new exterior color complement each other or clash is for you to decide.

Multicolor

It may seem natural to include both colors when repainting a vehicle that originally had a two-tone paint scheme. However, you should study your vehicle very closely before removing or priming over any of the existing paint. Where does the primary color stop and the secondary color start? Is there a piece of trim that covers this seam, and will that trim piece still be used after the paint job? Does the trim cover the entire paint seam, or is some of it left out in the open? What color are the doorjambs? How well you duplicate the original color transitions will have a great impact on your overall paint job, and it's better to end up with a high-quality monochrome paint job than a mediocre two-tone result.

Think about how you would mask the area where you are applying a different color and recognize that it should be the same on both sides of the vehicle. This will help you realize that you should take advantage of bodylines and natural breaks if you are designing a two-tone paint scheme. If you are going to be hiding a paint seam under a piece of trim, be sure to split the width of the trim evenly with each color. If the trim is an inch wide, this leaves a half inch for each color. You should be able to align the trim accurately enough to cover this; however, if the trim is narrower, you will have less room for error in masking or trim installation.

It doesn't really matter which color in a two-tone paint scheme you paint first. That said, plan ahead to make your masking work easier. Once all of the bodywork is done, the sealer has been applied, and all areas that are not to receive any paint masked off, no additional masking should be necessary for the first color application. Following this step, all areas with the first color must be masked off before the second color can be applied. For this reason, it makes sense to spray the color to the area that is going to be easiest to mask first, whether it is the lighter or darker color.

For example, if you are repainting a large four-door sedan that will be maroon with a dark gray secondary color below a bodyline running approximately through the middle of the doors, you could easily paint the lower area, mask it off, then paint the rest of the car. This will be an easier scenario than painting the top of the car, then trying to mask off the larger area below.

PAINT TYPE

Although paint application basics remain at least somewhat constant, the types of paint available have changed greatly over the years. The cheap and easy-to-use acrylic lacquer paint from a few decades ago is no longer available. Likewise, plain old "one-coat" acrylic enamel is gone as well. While those products were a snap to use, their replacements are far superior in finish quality, durability, and ease of handling.

continued on page 190

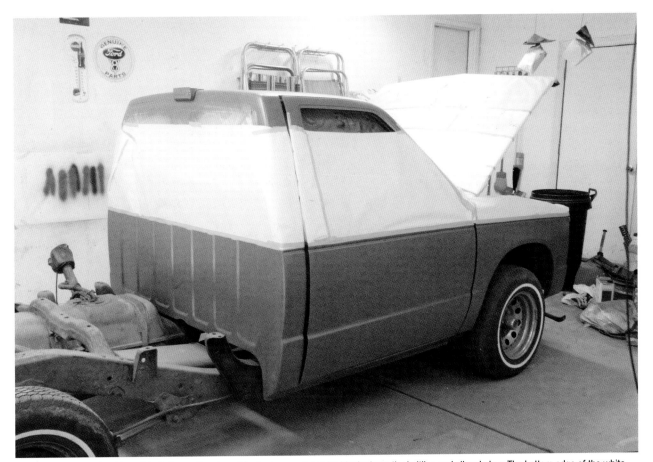

On this S-15, the sealer (shown) is dark gray in color, while the top coats will be black above the beltline and silver below. The bottom edge of the white masking paper will be the top line of the silver paint. Masking paper will prevent silver from landing on the glass, while a good aim will keep it off the top of the vehicle.

PAINTING: COLOR & OTHER TOP COATS

187

The silver is then sprayed on the area below the beltline.

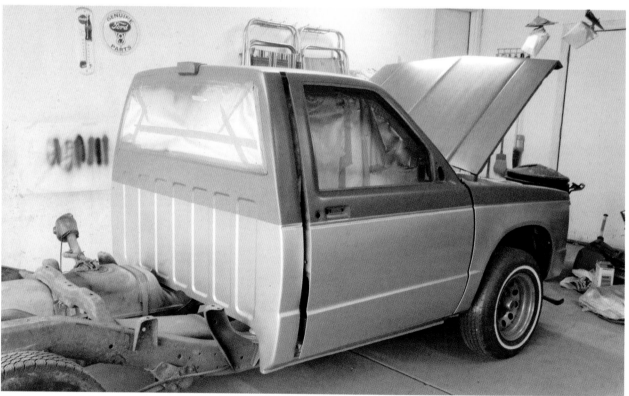

After the proper flash time, the masking material can be removed, revealing the final coats of silver on the lower portion of the truck. The dark gray visible in this photo is still the sealer, onto which black top coats will be applied.

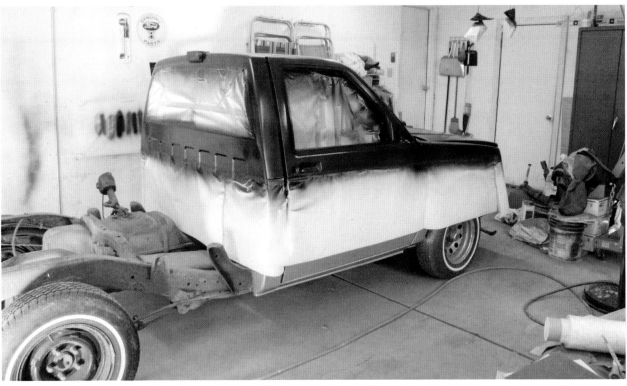

After applying masking to protect the fresh (yet dry) silver paint on the lower portion of the vehicle, black top coats are applied to the upper portion.

After the proper flash time, all masking is removed to reveal the silver and black paint combination. A red pinstripe will be applied to "finish" the paint edge.

continued from page 187

Single-Stage

Urethane enamel paint products (AKA single-stage) consist of a color pigment (paint) to which a prescribed amount of hardener is mixed just before application. By applying two or three coats of urethane enamel, a properly prepared surface will yield a high-gloss finish without buffing and will provide a very durable surface. The downside of this treatment is that there are fewer layers of material between your vehicle's body and the sometimes harsh elements it encounters. In other words, a scratch in the paint layer could easily expose the primer or even the bare metal, making it susceptible to rust formation.

Some painters believe a single-stage paint system that is wet sanded and buffed provides a better color. This may be true, as many people feel that the clear of a base coat/clear coat system takes away some of the appearance of depth that was common in the old lacquer paint jobs. As noted, the single-stage paint system leaves a layer of paint on the vehicle that will get thinner every time you rub it with a washing sponge, chamois, or wax applicator.

Base Coat/Clear Coat

If you are painting anything other than a one-color paint job, your job will be a lot easier if you use a base coat/clear coat paint system. Such a system will allow you to apply two coats of clear over the first color in a multicolor paint scheme. If you inadvertently miss any of the first color when you are masking, slight overspray from the second color can be sanded out of the clear protects the first color. After applying the second color (or third), the entire vehicle should be coated with two or three additional coats of clear.

Whether you are spraying one color or several, using a base coat/clear coat system involves more spraying time, since you must apply the base coat in enough coats to obtain coverage, and then the desired number of clear coats. You must allow the proper flash time between coats, but then you have to wait the proper amount of time for the base coat to dry before applying the clear. Product information sheets for your specific paint products will provide all of the flash time, dry time, and application pressure information that you need. Make sure that you ask for all available information when purchasing your paint products.

After you apply the clear coat and it has had an adequate time to dry, it can be wet sanded to remove any surface imperfections. Removing these imperfections will make the surface more optically flat, which is what provides the basis for the ultimate shine.

Tri-stage

Originally reserved for custom and high-end vehicles, tri-stage paint systems are becoming common on more widely available OEM paint finishes. Some exotic colors, such as pearls and candies, can be created by combining a base coat, color coat, and clear coat.

Base coats are usually a metallic color, such as gold or silver, but they can also be black or white. The color coat can be virtually any color, but it will vary in appearance depending on the base color to which it is applied. For example, a red color coat sprayed over a silver base will yield a different tint than if it is applied to a gold base coat. The clear coat finish will prevent wet sanding or polishing from distorting the blended color achieved between the base coat and color coat.

When you apply multiple coats of three different products, the amount of time required when using a tri-stage paint system increases considerably. As such, this system is not recommended for the beginner; however, if you're doing repair work on a vehicle with a tri-stage paint surface, it is the only way to complete your paint job.

APPLYING PAINT

Once you have decided what color to paint everything, you've purchased your paint and completed masking off, you are finally able to start applying paint. Well, almost. Have you actually sprayed any color before? If, for some reason, the paint is a different consistency and requires different air pressure than primer, there will be a slight difference in spraying the two. Using the same speed of movement and distance from the surface will work fine for one, but will have you wiping off runs and sags for the other.

Do-it-yourselfers must rely on personal practice and trial-and-error experience. If you haven't sprayed actual paint or if it has been a while, get an old hood, trunk lid, or door and practice before you turn your spray gun on your newly repaired bodywork. Mix paint products according to label instructions and apply them at the recommended air pressure.

Try painting with different fan patterns and pressure settings to see which combinations work best for intricate work in confined spaces, and which perform better on large panels. Practice holding the spray gun perpendicular to the work surface and see what happens when you don't. Use cans of inexpensive paint, and practice until you become familiar with the techniques required for good paint coverage.

Before You Start Spraying

In the paint booth or garage, wipe off body surfaces with a tack cloth as a final cleaning chore just before spraying any paint product. These specially made cloths are designed to pick up and retain very small specks of lint, dust, and other particles. Although wax and grease removers work well to get rid of contaminants like wax and grease, tack cloths work best for removing tiny pieces of cloth fiber and other items that could easily cause imperfections in paint finishes. Take the tack cloth out of the package, open it fully, and let it air out before using. Go over every square inch of body surface that will be exposed to paint product application to ensure that all traces of lint are removed. This should guarantee that debris is not blown over onto painted surfaces during the paint process.

Tack cloths have a limited lifespan, so refer to the instructions on their packaging to determine how many times they can be used effectively. Don't try to get more out of them than they are designed for. Once tack cloths are saturated with lint, debris, and residue, they will no longer pick up new material. In fact, they may spread accumulated materials absorbed from other cleaning jobs.

Applying Color

There are two basic philosophies when applying paint, and both have their respective advantages and disadvantages. Much of the decision will be based on how much of the vehicle is going to be repainted, how much has been disassembled for repair/replacement, and how soon you need to be able to drive the vehicle. Neither method is right or wrong, so it doesn't really matter which you choose.

Many builders of body-off restorations or show-oriented vehicles assemble all of the sheet metal completely to verify proper fit. The sheet metal is then disassembled as completely as possible, prepped,

Rather than installing freshly painted parts with the ever-present risk of damaging them during the process, many painters will apply paint to only the door jambs and other edges that would be difficult to paint after installation. Then, the vehicle is reassembled and everything that is left is painted in its installed position.

painted, and reassembled for the last time. This allows for thorough accessibility during the prep and painting stages, requiring minimal masking, but it also calls for extreme care during reassembly. Any nicks or scratches to the paint during assembly will require touchup. Also, since various components may be painted at different times, some subtle differences may appear from one component to another.

Other builders choose to prep and paint the underneath sides and edges of hoods, doors, and deck lids, along with the edges of fenders. The vehicle is then completely assembled, taking care not to damage any of the painted surfaces. After being assembled, the already painted surfaces are masked off and the entire vehicle painted at one time. This method calls for more masking, but it requires only minimal touchup (if any) and provides uniform color on adjacent panels.

Applying Clear Coat

The application of clear coat is no different from the process used for any other paint, except that it dries to a nearly invisible finish. Because of this, you must maintain a closer eye on your work so that each pass is made uniformly.

Instructions for mixing in solvents and hardeners with clear paint material are provided on product labels, application guides, and information sheets. It is critical to know the flash time between the last color coat and the application of clear. Spraying clear coats on before the solvents in color coats have sufficiently evaporated will cause checking and crazing.

AFTER APPLYING PAINT

Now that the paint has been applied, you are certainly much closer to being finished than when you first started, but there is still more work to do. At a minimum, you need to clean all of your spraying equipment and remove masking material from the vehicle. For a higher quality finish, if that is your intent, you will also need to wet sand any slight imperfections and buff the paint.

Cleaning Your Spray Equipment

For paint-spraying equipment to function properly, it must be kept clean, as the air and material passages are very small and can easily become permanently clogged. Check your local ordinances for disposing paint materials and follow the appropriate measures. The general procedure for cleaning spray equipment is to pour any unused material into a container that is suitable for

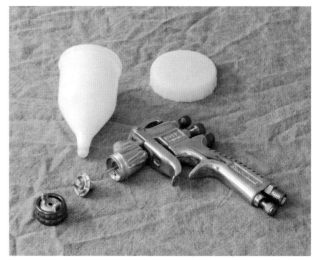

After emptying the paint cup and spraying clean thinner through the gun, disassemble it to clean each individual piece. In addition to this amount of disassembly, you should also remove the air control knob from the back of the gun and pull out the needle so that it can be cleaned. Put small parts in a cup with thinner to soak while you are wiping down the larger parts. When it is all reassembled, reconnect an air hose and blow dry air through the gun to expel any residual cleaning thinner from the internal passages.

disposal according to the requirements in your area. Then fill the paint cup about halfway full of the appropriate reducer for the material that you last sprayed. Spray this reducer at about 40 psi, gently shaking the spray gun occasionally to aid in removing partially dry material from the paint cup. Continue this procedure until only reducer comes out of the spray gun. Next, use a disposable towel dipped in reducer to wipe out the paint cup so that it has no traces of primer, paint, or clear in it. Remove the fluid tip from the front of the spray gun, wipe the area clean with a disposable towel dipped in reducer. Now reinstall the fluid tip and fill the cup about a third full of reducer again, and spray this all out until the spray gun is empty. Continue to blow air through the spray gun for a minute or two to help remove any reducer from the fluid passages.

Removing Masking Material

As anxious as you will be to see your vehicle with its new paint, be careful as you remove the masking material. If you simply tear off the masking paper and tape with reckless abandon, you will probably damage the new paint, since some amount of paint (color or clear) overlaps the edge of the masking tape. If the masking tape is simply pulled straight up from the painted surface, the paint will tend to flake along the edge. To prevent this from happening, pull the tape away from the freshly painted surface and back on itself so that the tape leaves the surface at a sharp angle.

If several coats of color and clear have been applied to the body surface, it may be necessary to cut through the layers of paint physically, at the edge of the tape. If you need to do this, make sure to use a sharp razorblade, take your time, and be careful. You don't want to damage the paint or give yourself a nasty cut.

Wet Sanding

Wet sanding (sometimes called "color sanding") is done after the paint has had sufficient time to cure. This removes any texture in the paint application, yielding a mirror-like finish. Always check with your paint supplier to verify that the paint you are using is compatible with wet sanding, as this is not the case for all paint. While urethane enamel can be wet sanded and buffed, just like clear, many of the older enamel products should not be wet sanded. As a basic rule of thumb, most catalyzed paint products (which contain a hardener added when the paint is mixed with reducer, prior to application)

can be wet sanded and buffed. As some products can be buffed after just 24 hours, and others require 90 days, be sure to verify the requirements for the paint you use with your paint supplier.

Base coat/clear coat or tri-stage paint systems are the typical candidates for wet sanding, as the sanding can be done on the clear, rather than on actual color coats. No sanding should be done to color coats in these systems, except for removing runs, drips, or other flaws in the coat. However, sanding out these defects may necessitate repainting an entire panel. Especially with candy finishes, sanding directly on the color surface will distort the tint and cause a visible blemish. Your wet sanding efforts should be concentrated on clear coats in order to avoid disturbing the underlying color coats. Wet sanding clear coats will bring out a much deeper shine and gloss when followed by controlled buffing and polishing.

Painters use very fine, 800- to 3000-grit sandpaper with water to smooth or remove minor blemishes on cured paint finishes that are designed to allow wet sanding. As with all other sanding tasks, you should use a sanding block. Since nibs of dirt or dust are small, fold sandpaper around a wooden paint stir stick

These two doors from the same vehicle show the difference between the wet sanding and buffing steps. The door nearest the camera has been wet sanded, as evidenced by the dull look. The door farthest away has been wet sanded and buffed to bring out the luster. As smooth as the doors may be prior to being painted, the actual application of paint will usually result in some amount of texture, commonly known as orange peel. Wet sanding (very light pressure with extremely fine sandpaper and lots of water) can smooth out the finished surface, which is what gives the extensive shine.

instead of using a large hand block for this task. The size is great for smoothing small spots and, since the width of ordinary wood stir sticks is about an inch, the area covered is limited to just what is needed. Only a small amount of pressure is required for this type of delicate sanding. Be sure to dip sandpaper in a bucket of water frequently to keep the paint surface wet and reduce the amount of material buildup on the sandpaper. A small amount of mild car washing soap should be added to the water bucket to provide lubrication for the sandpaper. Soak the sandpaper in water for 15 minutes before wet sanding. By letting the water sit in a bucket overnight, any minerals in the water that could cause scratches will have a chance to settle to the bottom.

For some finishes, such as those found on show cars, the entire car body may be wet sanded to bring out the richest, deepest, and most lustrous shine possible. Because they anticipate extensive wet sanding and polishing operations, painters of these cars make sure that they have applied plenty of clear coats. If they haven't, wet sanding will surely remove all of the thin clear coat material and eventually reach actual color coats, destroying an otherwise fine paint job.

To remove evidence of wet sanding, finishes are rubbed out or buffed with fine compound. This

Whether used with a base coat/clear coat system or a tri-coat system, which are wet sanded, or with a single-stage paint, buffing will provide the ultimate shine to the finish with everything else being equal. It is critical to pan ahead so that color coats and clear, if used, are thick enough to allow for buffing. The common mistake made while buffing is to burn through the paint, which requires paint touchup to correct.

work also brings out more shine and luster as well as flattening slight hints of orange peel. For spot painting or single-panel jobs, polishing adjacent body sections may be necessary to bring their lightly oxidized surfaces back to the point where they shine as brilliantly as a new paint job.

As meticulous as you were while masking, there may be a few body parts that exhibit signs of overspray. Before replacing all of the dismantled exterior body parts, consider removing obvious overspray and then repainting those affected areas with a proper color. In some areas, such as on fender wells, you could get away with just new coats of black paint or undercoating material. A task of this nature would be easier to accomplish while masking is still in place on the vehicle.

Buffing

As with wet sanding, you should check first with your paint supplier to verify that the paint system you are using is compatible with buffing and their specific buffing instructions. In the case of single-stage urethane, buffing new paint with gritty compound will actually dull the surface and ruin the finish. On the other hand, base coat/clear coat or tri-stage systems will benefit greatly from buffing, and the result will be a more brilliant finish with a much deeper shine.

Some buffing compounds are designed for use by hand, while others are designed to be used with a buffing machine. There are also different types of buffing pads, mainly foam or cloth. Some compounds should be used with a foam pad and a higher speed, while others call for a wool pad and a slower speed.

Rubbing compounds are made of relatively coarse polishing material and are designed to quickly remove minor blemishes and flatten the paint finish. As mentioned above, "flatten" in this instance means to make the painted finish as perfect as possible so that it is more reflective. Since this rubbing compound is coarse, it will leave light scratches or swirls on the painted surface. A much finer buffing compound should then be used to eliminate these fine swirls.

As refinishing products have changed over the years, so too have some of the methods for buffing. With new urethane paint products, many painters perform their first polishing with a 2,000-grit compound and a foam pad. This usually minimizes swirls and provides a satisfactory finish the first time around. If swirls are still present, these painters go back to a slightly coarser compound to remove swirls, then use the finer 2,000-grit again. Older technology—and what we all learned in junior high wood shop regarding sandpaper—would have called for a coarse rubbing compound, followed by finer stuff, instead of this seemingly backward procedure.

To use a buffer, first spread out a few strips of compound, each about 4 to 6 inches apart to cover an area no bigger than two square feet. Operate the buffing pad on top of a compound strip and work it over the strip's area, gradually moving down to pick up successive strips. The idea is to buff a 2-square-foot area while not allowing the pad to become dry. Continue buffing on that section until the compound is gone and the paint is shiny, then move on to another area. Keep the buffer moving to avoid burning into or even through the paint; be especially careful of this near ridges and corners.

If you are using buffing compound that can be applied by hand, use a back-and-forth motion. This will help prevent swirls and, when you're buffing by hand, you should do whatever you can to minimize your work.

Remove dried compound from the buffing pad by using a pad spur. Do this by gently but securely pushing a spur into the pad's nap while the pad is spinning. This breaks the dried compound loose and forces it out of the pad. Just be sure to clean the pad away from your car and anything else that you don't want covered with compound or pad lint.

Chapter 10
Reassembly

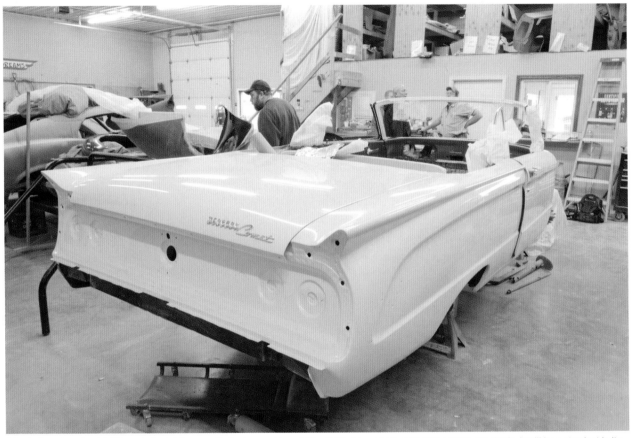

After bodywork and paint, this early Ford Falcon awaits final assembly and trim. While it is nothing radical by today's standards, it will be a standout in its tasteful simplicity.

By now you should be seeing some light at the end of the tunnel. All of the once-damaged parts should be repaired or replaced and refinished in the appropriate color. Any blemishes have been wet sanded, polished, and touched up. The masking material is removed and you just need to reassemble everything. Much of this will be reinstalling the various pieces and parts that are not sheet metal, such as lights and trim.

Installing various parts on car bodies must be done systematically, in much the same way they were dismantled. Certain trim sections are designed to be installed first, with part of their edge covered by the next section. Failure to follow an intended sequence the first time will require you to take off those out-of-order sections and put them back

on correctly. This not only creates extra work, it also increases the chances for scratching or nicking the vehicle's new paint.

There is no immediacy surrounding the detailing or reinstallation of dismantled parts—except the excitement at being finished with your project. Even though it may have been an enjoyable process, you are probably ready to be done. After all, other projects are likely waiting for you around the house.

Regardless of how fast or slow you want to proceed, take the time to carefully detail and assemble body parts so that they go on right the first time and look good once they are in place. This might be the last time you have the opportunity to thoroughly clean and detail dismantled parts. And, since they will be off the vehicle body, the jobs of cleaning, polishing, and waxing will not be hindered by their attachment to body panels or locations in confined spaces.

INSTALLING TRIM

Before reinstalling any pieces of trim that were removed, check to make sure that they aren't damaged and are clean and shiny. If the trim is metal, it will be easier to clean and polish if these tasks are done before reinstalling the trim. Plastic trim may be painted the same color as the body, and if so it should be checked for chips or other paint defects. If necessary, any damage should be touched up while the trim is still off the vehicle. Vinyl or rubber trim sections might be treated to a solid scrubbing with an all-purpose cleaner such as Simple Green and a soft brush. When they are dry, apply a satisfactory coat of vinyl dressing. Rub in the treatment with a soft cloth or a very soft brush. Be sure to wipe off all excess.

Make sure that all of the clips and retainers are on hand before attaching trim pieces. Make sure you fully understand how they are intended to work before forcing them on in an inappropriate manner, possibly breaking them in the process. As you did for their removal, have a helper assist you in replacing extra-long pieces. This will help prevent bends or wrinkles on the trim, and it also adds more control to the installation to prevent accidental scratches on paint finishes.

Since door handles and key locks attach directly to painted body panels, you should install them with care to avoid causing scratches, chips, or nicks to the finish. In many cases, gaskets or seals are designed for placement between hardware and body skin. If the old gasket is worn, cracked, or otherwise damaged, do not use it. Wait to install that handle or exterior door item until a new gasket is acquired.

The screws, nuts, or bolts used to secure door handles are normally accessed through openings on the interior sides of doors. You have to reach through with your hand to tighten the fasteners. Be sure to use wrenches or sockets of the correct size to make this awkward job as easy as possible. After handles and key locks are secured, attach linkages or cables that run to the actual latch mechanisms.

As with other exterior trim pieces and accessories, take this opportunity to clean, polish, and detail grille assemblies while they are off your car. Touch up paint nicks, clean tiny nooks and crannies, and wax metallic

Other than the raindrops on this hood trim, the chrome is in very good condition, even if the paint is wearing thin. The painted area could be scuffed with some 400-grit sandpaper, cleaned with wax and grease remover, then masked off and sprayed with the appropriate colors of touchup paint.

parts as necessary. Use a soft toothbrush and cotton swabs to reach into tight spaces. Should painted parts look old and worn, consider sanding and repainting them. Tiny chips or nicks can be touched up with the proper paint, using a fine artist's paintbrush.

A thorough cleaning with a soft toothbrush and mild cleaner should work well to remove accumulations of polish, wax, and dirt from tiny corners and designed impressions, making these items look like new. Be sure to check that their fastening mechanisms are intact. Plastic emblems are not always easy to remove, and many times their plastic pins or supports crack during dismantling. If yours are damaged, you may have to replace them with new ones.

GRAPHICS OR ARTWORK

Most graphics are applied in a completely separate operation from the painting process. Even though their use may be included in the beginning planning stages, their actual application takes place long after the spray guns have been cleaned and the masking paper removed. The paint that you so carefully applied needs sufficient time to cure fully, so you don't want to trap solvents beneath additional graphics.

Anytime you apply graphics or other artwork to your vehicle, a base coat/clear coat system for the entire car will make for easier repair should overspray or other miscues need to be sanded off. Most blemishes can be removed from the clear without affecting the color

This air vent cover is easy to reinstall: it simply snaps into place. It would most likely never be removed unless damaged in an accident, and then it would be replaced, as this one has been.

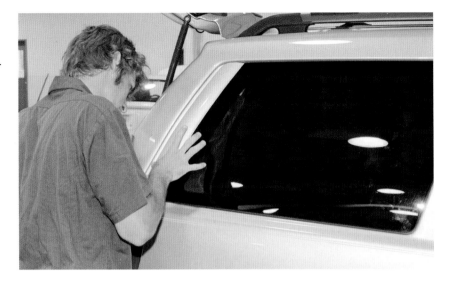

This cladding at the bottom of the door is commonly found on SUVs, often secured in place with a few rows of two-sided tape. There may or may not be alignment pins on this outer panel to align with small alignment holes on the door.

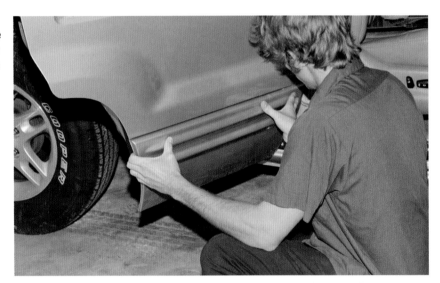

After verifying that the panel fits as desired, the protective cover is removed from the tape on the back of the panel, alignment pins aligned (if present), and the panel pressed firmly into place.

beneath it. However, if there is no clear from which to remove overspray, you can easily sand through the color right into primer.

Before adding any artwork, the entire area should be cleaned with wax and grease remover. Surface preparation will depend on the media being applied, so read the instructions provided or check with your paint and supply jobber.

Pinstriping

Pinstriping should be used as the finishing touch to any multicolor paint scheme if chrome or stainless trim is not used. Pinstriping can also be used as a standalone accent to a single-color paint scheme. However, a vehicle's profile can look too busy if pinstriping is used in conjunction with body side molding. Sometimes less looks much better.

Common on factory paint jobs, pinstriping is usually a single or double line, approximately ⅛ inch wide and running along the beltline or other bodyline of the vehicle, in a contrasting or complementary color. Since this application is as an accent, a bright color is common, such as an orange pinstripe on a maroon vehicle, or purple on a black vehicle. You most likely would not choose to apply a two-tone paint job to a vehicle using equal amounts of these two colors, but a pinstripe with a thin width can work well.

Graphics such as flames, scallops, or even lettering simply looks more complete if outlined with tasteful pinstriping. Also, a pinstripe can cover an otherwise unattractive seam of color where two colors abut each other in a multicolor paint job. Pinstriping can also serve to conceal slight irregularities in the edge of the paint that may have resulted from the removal of masking material. Whether necessary to hide miscues or not, no flame or scallop painting is considered to be complete unless it's pinstriped.

One-Shot Sign Painter's enamel is the most common paint for pinstriping or lettering. It is available from larger art supply stores, some auto body paint suppliers, or through mail order from the Eastwood Company. A relatively inexpensive product, this paint yields virtually any color with just a few primary colors and some extra mixing jars.

Before applying pinstriping paint, the target surface must be free of any contaminants, so apply a wax and grease remover with a clean cloth, then wipe it off with a second dry cloth. Painted pinstriping can be applied freehand by using a pinstriping brush (AKA

a "daggar") or a mechanical device, such as a Beugler pinstriping tool.

Although it does take a bit of practice, a Beugler pinstriping tool is much easier for the beginner to use for consistent results. This tool is a small canister filled with paint and a built-in wheel that transfers the paint to the surface. The width of the wheel determines the width of the stripe, while heads with two wheels provide two stripes. The tool can be used freehand, but it will also accept a guide arm that can be run alongside a magnetic guide that can be aligned on the vehicle's body as desired.

LONG-TERM PAINT CARE

Contemporary catalyzed paint products are much more durable and robust than the lacquer and enamel products used in the past. Still, don't expect the paint on your newly repaired body to shine forever without some routine maintenance. Washing, waxing, and occasional polishing are essential if you intend to keep that new car appearance. By keeping a good coat of high-quality wax on your vehicle's painted exterior surfaces, dirt and road debris are less likely to stick to the surface and will also make washing your vehicle easier.

Unless you are talking about a show-only vehicle that you seldom, if ever, drive, small nicks or chips will appear sooner or later. These blemishes should be repaired as soon as possible. If not, any exposed metal will begin to oxidize, which can spread under paint and damage adjacent metal panels. You have no doubt spent a significant amount of time and money repairing the damage to your vehicle, so try to maintain it with some simple but consistent maintenance.

Washing, Polishing, and Waxing

Car wash soap products can be found at auto parts stores and discount department stores. For the most part, almost any brand of car wash soap should be well suited for the finish on your vehicle. Just be sure to read the label for any warnings and to follow the mixing directions on labels of any product that you use.

The best way to prevent minute scratches or other blemishes on paint is to wash the vehicle in sections. Wash the dirtiest parts first, including the rocker panels, fender well lips, and lower front and rear end locations. Then thoroughly rinse your soft cotton wash mitt and wash soap bucket. Mix up a new batch of wash soap to clean the vehicle sides. If their condition was relatively clean to start with, you can

continued on page 202

HOW TO REPLACE OEM ADHESIVE GRAPHICS

Although trim, emblems, and badges on contemporary vehicles are usually made of plastic rather than the polished, chrome-plated metal of bygone years, it is still present in some form on most vehicles. Since it's plastic, the trim is usually adhesive-backed, rather than being bolted on. Mike at Jerry's Auto Body makes installing a new piece of trim on the rear quarter of an SUV look pretty simple.

1 From measuring the graphic on the other side of the vehicle, it was determined that the top of the emblem is ¾ inch below the bottom of the silver pinstripe. Coincidentally, ¾-inch masking tape is very common, so this emblem location is no surprise. As a guideline, a piece of ¾-inch masking tape is aligned at the bottom of the aforementioned pinstripe.

2 To ensure that the emblem adheres properly, a bit of wax and grease remover is sprayed onto the application area, then wiped off with a clean paper towel. This should remove anything that would prevent proper adhesion.

The protective backing is removed from the adhesive on back of the "4x4" emblem. The top of the emblem is then aligned with the lower edge of the masking tape and pressed into place.

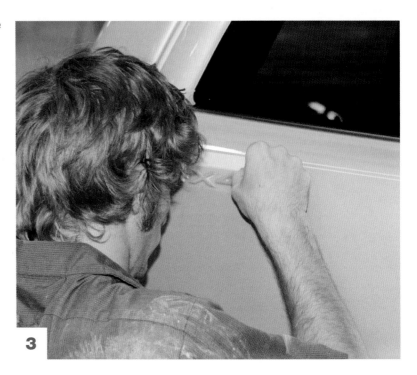

3

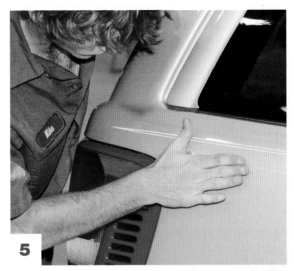

4

The masking tape used to align the emblem is peeled away.

5

Firm and even pressure is applied to the emblem to ensure that it adheres to the body surface.

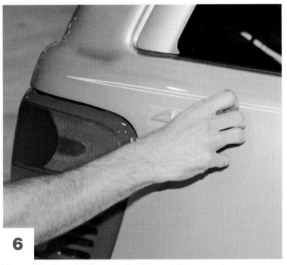

6

The emblem's protective covering is carefully removed.

7

After the protective cover is removed from the emblem, this portion of the vehicle looks just like it did when it was new.

Regardless of which products you use, most car care companies provide a full line of waxes and cleaners that are designed to work together for the best results. As with paint products, there really is no reason to mix and match components of the car care equation.

continued from page 199

continue with that bucket of sudsy water to wash the hood, roof, and trunk areas.

This process rids your wash mitt and bucket of dirt and other scratch hazards, like sand and road grit. If you were to wash your entire car with just one bucket of sudsy water, you would increase the chances of your wash mitt picking up debris from the bucket, which will then be rubbed against the vehicle's lustrous finish. Likewise, anytime you notice that your wash mitt is dirty, or if it falls to the ground, always rinse it off with clear water before dipping it into the wash bucket. This helps to keep the wash water clean and free of debris.

To clean inside tight spaces, such as window molding edges and louvers, use a soft, natural-hair floppy paintbrush. Don't use synthetic-bristled paintbrushes, as they can cause minute scratches on paint surfaces. In addition, wrap a thick layer of heavy duct tape over the paintbrush's metal band; this will help guard against paint scratches or nicks as you vigorously agitate the paintbrush in tight spaces, possibly knocking the brush into painted body parts such as those around headlights and grilles.

Polish and wax products seem to be one of the most confusing subjects regarding automotive finish maintenance for novice auto enthusiasts. Although both are designed as paint finish maintenance materials, each has its own separate purpose. Polishes clean paint finishes and remove accumulations of oxidation and

other contaminants. On the other hand, wax does no cleaning or shining. It does, however, protect paint finishes that have already been cleaned and polished. Simply stated, polish cleans—wax protects.

Auto body paint and supply stores generally carry the largest selection of auto polishes and waxes, although many auto parts stores stock good assortments. Every polish should include a definitive label that explains what kind of paint finish it is designed for, such as heavily oxidized, mildly oxidized, and new finish glaze. Those designed for heavy oxidation problems contain much coarser grit than those for new car finishes.

Along with descriptions of the kind of paint finish particular polishes are designed for, labels will also note which products are intended for use with a buffer. Those with heavy concentrations of coarse grit are not recommended for machine use. Their polishing strength, combined with the power of a buffer, could cause large-scale paint-burn problems.

Carnauba wax is perhaps the best product to use for protecting automobile paint finishes. Meguiar's, Eagle 1, and other manufacturers of cosmetic car care products offer auto enthusiasts an assortment of carnauba-based auto wax products. Other paint protection products on the market profess to work like wax, but they often contain different chemical bases; be sure you understand their correct application before putting them in contact with your new paint job.

Some, typically with "poly" or "polymer" in the product name, are loaded with silicone materials. Although they may protect your car's finish for a long time, professional auto painters advise against their use because the silicone content is so high and saturating that any repainting that may be required in the future may be plagued with severe fisheye problems. In some cases, silicones have been known to penetrate paint finishes and eventually become embedded in sheet metal panels.

If you find yourself in a quandary when it comes time to select a polish or wax product, seek advice from a knowledgeable auto body paint supplier. This person should have current information on the latest products from manufacturers and insight into user satisfaction from professional painters and detailers in the field.

When to Wash New Paint Finishes

Newer paints with hardener additives can generally be washed safely after one or two days, as long as mild automotive soap products are used and gentle washing efforts practiced. For uncatalyzed enamels, plenty of time (a few days or a week) should be allotted for paint solvents to evaporate or chemically react before washing newly sprayed car bodies. To be on the safe side, check with your paint supplier to verify the required waiting time for the paint products you have purchased.

How Long Before Waxing?

Light coats of quality auto wax actually form protective seals on top of paint finishes. Even though they are quite thin and by no means permanent, these wax seals will prevent solvent evaporation. Should that occur, vapors that should leave the paint can be trapped. Consequently, as confined vapors continue their evaporation activity and persist in seeking the open atmosphere, minute amounts of pressure build up. These can eventually cause damage in the form of blisters to the new paint finish. So, instead of protecting a paint surface, waxing too soon after new paint applications can actually cause unexpected damage.

You should wait at least 90 to 120 days before waxing your freshly painted vehicle. During the summer or in any locations where the weather is warm and humidity is relatively low, 90 days should allow plenty of time for paint solvents to evaporate completely. When the weather is cooler or more humid, it takes longer for the solvent in the paint to evaporate, making it necessary to wait longer before applying wax.

While you are waiting to apply a good coat of high-quality wax to the exterior, there are plenty of other things you can do to make your once crumpled car seem new again. Cleaning the windows inside and out, vacuuming the carpet, and cleaning the upholstery will make any vehicle more enjoyable to drive. Polish the chrome, scrub the tires, then clean the engine compartment and remove as much stuff as practical from the trunk.

Your once-damaged vehicle is looking good again. I knew you could do it.

Sources

Auto Metal Direct
940 Sherwin Parkway, Suite 180, Buford, GA 30518
www.autometaldirect.com
866-591-8309
Reproduction sheet metal and accessories

Campbell Hausfeld
100 Production Drive, Harrison, OH 45030
www.chpower.com
800-543-6400
Air compressors and pneumatic tools

Chief Automotive Systems
966 Industrial Drive, Madison, IN 47250
www.chiefautomotive.com
800-445-9262
Chassis and unibody straightening equipment

Danchuk Manufacturing
3201 S. Standard Avenue, Santa Ana, CA 92705
www.danchuk.com
800-648-9554, 714-751-1957
Chevrolet restoration parts

Dupli-Color Products
101 Prospect Avenue NW500 Republic, Cleveland, OH 44115
www.duplicolor.com
800-247-3270
Paint products

Dynacorn International Inc.
4030 Via Pescador, Camarillo, CA 93012
www.dynacorn.com
805-987-8818
Reproduction sheet metal and accessories

Eastwood Company
263 Shoemaker Road, Pottstown, PA 19464
www.eastwood.com
800-343-9353
Automotive restoration tools, equipment, and supplies

Goodmark Industries
www.goodmarkindustries.com
877-477-3577
Sheet metal replacement panels

Hemmings Motor News
P.O. Box 100, Bennington, VT 05201
www.hemmings.com
800-227-4373
Classified ads for vehicles, products, and services

High Ridge NAPA
2707 High Ridge Boulevard, High Ridge, MO 63049
636-677-6400
Automotive parts, paint products

HTP America
180 Joey Drive, Elk Grove Village, IL 60007
www.usaweld.com
800-872-9353, 847-357-0700
Welders, plasma cutters, tools, and accessories

Jerry's Auto Body Inc.
1399 Church Street, Union, MO 63084
636-583-4757
Auto body repair

Licari Auto Body Supply Inc.
2800 High Ridge Boulevard, High Ridge, MO 63049
636-677-1566
PPG paint products and supplies

Meguiars
17991 Mitchell South, Irvine, CA 92614-6015
www.meguiars.com
800-347-5700
Car care products

Miller Electric Manufacturing Company
1635 W. Spencer Street, Appleton, WI 54914-4911
www.millerwelds.com
800-426-4553, 920-734-9821
Welders, plasma cutters, tools, and accessories

Morfab Customs Inc.
506 Suite C, Terry Street, Washington, MO 63090
www.morfabcustoms.com
636-262-1268
Hot rod fabrication and assembly, welding, painting

Mothers Polish Company
5456 Industrial Drive, Huntington Beach, CA 92649-1519
www.mothers.com
714-891-3364
Polishes, waxes, and cleaners

Murrill's Classic Dreams
1871 Pottery Road, Suite 100, Washington, MO 63090
636-239-1240
Auto body repair

PPG Refinish Group
19699 Progress Drive, Strongsville, OH 44149
www.ppgrefinish.com
440-572-6880 fax
Paint products

Year One
P.O. Box 521, Braselton, GA 30517
www.yearone.com
800-932-7663
Automotive restoration parts

Index